MY
WONDERFUL
VISIT

Charlie Chaplin

[ZHINGOORA BOOKS]

This edition is published by
Zhingoora Books.

CONTENTS

My favourite autograph.

I.

I DECIDE TO PLAY HOOKEY

A steak-and-kidney pie, influenza, and a cablegram. There is the triple alliance that is responsible for the whole thing. Though there might have been a bit of homesickness and a desire for applause mixed up in the cycle of circumstances that started me off to Europe for a vacation.

For seven years I had been basking in California's perpetual sunlight, a sunlight artificially enhanced by the studio Cooper-Hewitts. For seven years I had been working and thinking along in a single channel and I wanted to get away. Away from Hollywood, the cinema colony, away from scenarios, away from the celluloid smell of the studios, away from contracts, press notices, cutting rooms, crowds, bathing beauties, custard pies, big shoes, and little moustaches. I was in the atmosphere of achievement, but an achievement which, to me, was rapidly verging on stagnation.

I wanted an emotional holiday. Perhaps I am projecting at the start a difficult condition for conception, but I assure you that even the clown has his rational moments and I needed a few.

The triple alliance listed above came about rather simultaneously. I had finished the picture of "The Kid" and "The Idle Class" and was about to embark on another. The company had been engaged. Script and settings were ready. We had worked on the picture one day.

I was feeling very tired, weak, and depressed. I had just recovered from an attack of influenza. I was in one of those "what's the use" moods. I wanted something and didn't know what it was.

And then Montague Glass invited me to dinner at his home in Pasadena. There were many other invitations, but this one carried with it the assurance that there would be a steak-and-kidney pie. A weakness of mine. I was on hand ahead of time. The pie was a symphony. So was the evening. Monty Glass, his charming wife, their little daughter, Lucius Hitchcock, the illustrator, and his wife—just a homey little family party devoid of red lights and jazz orchestras. It awoke within me a chord of something reminiscent. I couldn't quite tell what.

After the final onslaught on the pie, into the parlour before an open fire. Conversation, not studio patois nor idle chatter. An exchange of ideas—ideas founded on ideas. I discovered that Montague Glass was much more than the author of *Potash and Perlmutter*. He thought. He was an accomplished musician.

He played the piano. I sang. Not as an exponent of entertainment, but as part of the group having a pleasant, homey evening. We played charades. The evening was over too soon. It left me wishing. Here was home in its true sense. Here was a man artistically and commercially successful who still managed to lock the doors and put out the cat at night.

I drove back to Los Angeles. I was restless. There was a cablegram waiting for me from London. It called attention to the fact that my latest picture, "The Kid," was about to make its appearance in London, and, as it had been acclaimed my best, this was the time for me to make the trip back to my native land. A trip that I had been promising myself for years.

What would Europe look like after the war?

I thought it over. I had never been present at the first showing of one of my pictures. Their début to me had been in Los Angeles projection rooms. I had been missing something vital and stimulating. I had success, but it was stored away somewhere. I had never opened the package and tasted it. I sort of wanted to be patted on the back. And I rather relished the pats coming in and from England. They had hinted that I could, so I wanted to turn London upside down. Who wouldn't want to do that? And all the time there was the spectre of nervous breakdown from overwork threatening and the results of influenza apparent, to say nothing of the steak-and-kidney pie.

Sensation of the pleasantest sort beckoned me, at the same time rest was promised. I wanted to grab it while it was good. Perhaps "The Kid" might be my last picture. Maybe there would never be another chance for me to bask in the spotlight. And I wanted to see Europe—England, France, Germany, and Russia. Europe was new.

It was too much. I stopped preparations on the picture we were taking. Decided to leave the next night for Europe. And did it despite the protests and the impossibility howlers. Tickets were taken. We packed; everyone was shocked. I was glad of it. I wanted to shock everyone.

The next night I believe that most of Hollywood was at the train in Los Angeles to see me off. And so were their sisters and their cousins and their aunts. Why was I going? A secret mission, I told them. It was an effective answer. I was immediately under contract to do pictures in Europe in the minds of most of them. But then, would they have believed or understood if I had told them I wanted an emotional holiday? I don't believe so.

There was the usual station demonstration at the train. The crowd rather surprised me. It was but a foretaste. I do not try to remember the shouted messages of cheer that were flung at me. They were of the usual sort, I imagine. One, however, sticks. My brother Syd at the last moment rushed up to one of my party.

"For God's sake, don't let him get married!" he shouted.

It gave the crowd a laugh and me a scare.

The train pulled out and I settled down to three days of relaxation and train routine. I ate sometimes in the dining car, sometimes in our drawing-room. I slept atrociously. I always do. I hate travelling. The faces left on the platform at Los Angeles began to look kinder and more attractive. They did not seem the sort to drive one away. But they had, or maybe it was optical illusion on my part, illusion fostered by mental unrest.

For two thousand miles we did the same thing over many times, then repeated it. Perhaps there were many interesting people on the train. I did not find out. The percentage of interesting ones on trains is too small to hazard. Most of the time we played solitaire. You can play it many times in two thousand miles.

Then we reached Chicago. I like Chicago, I have never been there for any great length of time, but my glimpses of it have disclosed tremendous activity. Its record speaks achievement.

But to me, personally, Chicago suggested Carl Sandburg, whose poetry I appreciate highly and whom I had met in Los Angeles. I must see dear old Carl and also call at the office of the *Daily News*. They were running an enormous scenario contest. I am one of the judges, and it happens that Carl Sandburg is on the same paper.

Our party went to the Blackstone Hotel, where a suite had been placed at our disposal. The hotel management overwhelmed us with courtesies.

Then came the reporters. You can't describe them unless you label them with the hackneyed interrogation point.

"Mr. Chaplin, why are you going to Europe?"

"Just for a vacation."

"Are you going to make pictures while you are there?"

"No."

"What do you do with your old moustaches?"

"Throw them away."

"What do you do with your old canes?"

"Throw them away."

"What do you do with your old shoes?"

"Throw them away."

That lad did well. He got in all those questions before he was shouldered aside and two black eyes boring through lenses surrounded by tortoise-shell frames claimed an innings. I restored the "prop grin" which I had decided was effective for interviews.

"Mr. Chaplin, have you your cane and shoes with you?"

"No."

"Why not?"

"I don't think I'll need them."

"Are you going to get married while you are in Europe?"

"No."

THE CALIFORNIAN SEA LION
THE ORIGIN OF THE FAMOUS BOOTS REVEALED AT LAST.
(*One of my favourite cartoons.*)

The bespectacled one passed with the tide. As he passed I let the grin slip away, but only for a moment. Hastily I recalled it as a charming young lady caught me by the arm.

"Mr. Chaplin, do you ever expect to get married?"

"Yes."

"To whom?"

"I don't know."

"Do you want to play 'Hamlet'?"

"Why, I don't know. I haven't thought much about it, but if you think there are any reasons why——"

But she was gone. Another district attorney had the floor.

"Mr. Chaplin, are you a Bolshevik?"

"No."

"Then why are you going to Europe?"

"For a holiday."

"What holiday?"

"Pardon me, folks, but I did not sleep well on the train and I must go to bed."

Like a football player picking a hole in the line, I had seen the bedroom door open and a friendly hand beckon. I made for it. Within I had every opportunity to anticipate the terror that awaited me on my holiday. Not the crowds. I love them. They are friendly and instantaneous. But interviewers! Then we went to the *News* office, and the trip was accomplished without casualty. There we met photographers. I didn't relish facing them. I hate still pictures.

But it had to be done. I was the judge in the contest and they must have pictures of the judge.

Now I had always pictured a judge as being a rather dignified personage, but I learned about judges from them. Their idea of the way to photograph a judge was to have him standing on his head or with one leg pointing east. They suggested a moustache, a Derby hat, and a cane.

It was inevitable.

I couldn't get away from Chaplin.

And I did so want a holiday.

But I met Carl Sandburg. There was an oasis amid the misery. Good old Carl! We recalled the days in Los Angeles. It was a most pleasant chat.

Back to the hotel.

Reporters. More reporters. Lady reporters.

A publicity barrage.

"Mr. Chaplin—"

But I escaped. What a handy bedroom! There must be something in practice. I felt that I negotiated it much better on the second attempt. I rather wanted to try out my theory to see if I had become an adept in dodging into the bedroom. I would try it. I went out to brave the reporters. But they were gone. And when I ducked back into the bedroom, as a sort of rehearsal, it fell flat. The effect was lost without the cause.

A bit of food, some packing, and then to the train again. This time for New York. Crowds again. I liked them. Cameras. I did not mind them this time, as I was not asked to pose.

Carl was there to see me off.

I must do or say something extra nice to him. Something he could appreciate. I couldn't think. I talked inanities and I felt that he knew I was being inane. I tried to think of a passage of his poetry to recite. I couldn't. Then it came—the inspiration.

"Where can I buy your book of poems, Carl?" I almost blurted it out. It was gone. Too late to be recalled.

"At any bookstore."

His reply may have been casual. To me it was damning.

Ye gods, what a silly imbecile I was! I needed rest. My brain was gone. I couldn't think of a thing to say in reprieve. Thank God, the train pulled out then. I hope Carl will understand and forgive when he reads this, if he ever does.

A wretched sleep *en train*, more solitaire, meals at schedule times, and then we hit New York.

Crowds. Reporters. Photographers. And Douglas Fairbanks. Good old Doug. He did his best, but Doug has never had a picture yet where he had to buck news photographers. They snapped me in every posture anatomically possible. Two of them battled with my carcass in argument over my facing east or west.

Neither won. But I lost. My body couldn't be split. But my clothes could—and were.

But Doug put in a good lick and got me into an automobile. Panting, I lay back against the cushions.

To the Ritz went Doug and I.

To the Ritz went the crowd.

Or at least I thought so, for there was a crowd there and it looked like the same one. I almost imagined I saw familiar faces. Certainly I saw cameras. But this time our charge was most successful. With a guard of porters as shock troops, we negotiated the distance between the curb and the lobby without the loss of a single button.

I felt rather smart and relieved. But, as usual, I was too previous. We ascended to the suite. There they were. The gentlemen of the press. And one lady of the press.

"Mr. Chaplin, why are you going to Europe?"

"For a vacation."

"What do you do with your old moustaches?"

"Throw them away."

"Do you ever expect to get married?"

"Yes."

"What's her name?"

"I don't know."

"Are you a Bolshevik?"

"I am an artist. I am interested in life. Bolshevism is a new phase of life. I must be interested in it."

"Do you want to play 'Hamlet'?"

"Why, I don't know—"

Again Lady Luck flew to my side. I was called to the telephone. I answered the one in my bedroom, and closed the door, and kept it closed. The Press departed. I felt like a wrung dish-rag. I looked into the mirror. I saw a Cheshire cat grinning back at me. I was still carrying the "prop" grin that I had invented for interviews. I wondered if it would be easier to hold it all the time rather than chase it into play at the sight of reporters. But some one might accuse me of imitating Doug. So I let the old face slip back to normal.

Doug came. Mary was better. She was with him. It was good to see her. The three of us went to the roof to be photographed. We were, in every conceivable pose until some one suggested that Doug should hang over the edge of the roof, holding Mary in one hand and me in the other. Pretty little thought. But that's as far as it got. I beat Doug to the refusal by a hair.

It's great to have friends like Doug and Mary. They understood me perfectly. They knew what the seven years' grind had meant to my nerves. They knew just how badly I needed this vacation, how I needed to get away from studios and pictures, how I needed to get away from myself.

Doug had thought it all out and had planned that while I was in New York my vacation should be perfect. He would see that things were kept pleasant for me.

So he insisted that I should go and see his new picture, "The Three Musketeers.

I was nettled. I didn't want to see pictures. But I was polite. I did not refuse, though I did try to evade.

It was useless. Very seriously he wanted me to see the picture and give my honest opinion. He wanted my criticism, my suggestions.

I had to do it. I always do. I saw the picture in jerks.

Reporters were there. Their attendance was no secret.

The picture over, I suggested a few changes and several cuts which I thought would improve it.

I always do.

They listened politely and then let the picture ride the way it was.

They always do.

Fortunately, the changes I suggested were not made, and the picture is a tremendous success.

But I still have status as a critic. I am invited to a showing of Mary's picture, "Little Lord Fauntleroy," and asked for suggestions. They know that I'll criticise. I always do and they are afraid of me. Though when they look at my pictures they are always kind and sympathetic and never criticise.

I told Mary her picture was too long. I told her where to cut it. Which, of course, she doesn't do. She never does.

She and Doug listen politely and the picture stands. It always does.

Newspaper men are at the hotel. I go through the same barrage of questions. My "prop" grin does duty for fifteen minutes. I escape.

Douglas 'phones me. He wants to be nice to me. I am on my vacation and he wants it to be a very pleasant one. So he invites me to see "The Three Musketeers" again. This time at its first showing before the public.

Before the opening of Doug's picture we were to have dinner together, Mary and Doug, Mrs. Condé Nast and I.

I felt very embarrassed at meeting Mrs. Nast again. Somewhere there lurks in my memory a broken dinner engagement. It worried me, as I had not even written. It was so foolish not to write. I would be met probably with an "all-is-forgiven" look.

I decide that my best defence is to act vague and not speak of it. I do so and get away with it.

And she has the good taste not to mention it, so a pleasant time is had by all.

We went to the theatre in Mrs. Nast's beautiful limousine. The crowds were gathered for several blocks on every side of the theatre.

I felt proud that I was in the movies. Though on this night, with Douglas and Mary, I felt that I was trailing in their glory. It was their night.

There are cheers—for Mary, for Doug, for me. Again I feel proud that I am in the movies. I try to look dignified. I coax up the "prop" smile and put into it real pleasure. It is a real smile. It feels good and natural.

We get out of the car and crowds swarm. Most of the "all-American" selections are there. Doug takes Mary under his wing and ploughs through as though he were doing a scene and the crowd were extras.

I took my cue from him. I took Mrs. Nast's arm. At least I tried to take it, but she seemed to sort of drift away from me down towards Eighth Avenue, while I, for no apparent reason, backed toward Broadway. The tide changed. I was swept back toward the entrance of the theatre. I was not feeling so proud as I had been. I was still smiling at the dear public, but it had gone back to the "prop" smile.

I realised this and tried to put real pleasure into the smile again. As the grin broadened it opened new space and a policeman parked his fist in it.

I don't like the taste of policemen's fists. I told him so. He glared at me and pushed me for a "first down." My hat flew toward the heavens. It has never returned to me.

I felt a draught. I heard machinery. I looked down. A woman with a pair of scissors was snipping a piece from the seat of my trousers. Another grabbed my tie and almost put an end to my suffering through strangulation. My collar was next. But they only got half of that.

My shirt was pulled out. The buttons torn from my vest. My feet trampled on. My face scratched. But I still retained the smile, "prop" one though it was. Whenever I could think of it I tried to raise it above the level of a "prop" smile and was always rewarded with a policeman's fist. I kept insisting that I was Charlie Chaplin and that I belonged inside. It was absolutely necessary that I should see "The Three Musketeers."

Insistence won. As though on a prearranged signal I felt myself lifted from my feet, my body inverted until my head pointed toward the centre of the lobby and my feet pointed toward an electric sign advertising the Ziegfeld Roof. Then there was a surge, and I moved forward right over the heads of the crowd through the lobby.

As I went through the door, not knowing into what, I saw a friend.

With the "prop" smile still waving, I flung back, "See you later," and, head first, I entered the theatre and came to in a heap at the foot of a bediamonded dowager. I looked up, still carrying the "prop" smile, but my effort fell flat. There was no applause in the look she gave me.

Crestfallen, I gathered myself together, and with what dignity there was left I strode to the box that had been set aside for our party. There was Mary, as sweet and beautiful as ever; Mrs. Nast, calm and composed: Doug serene and dapper.

"Late again," they looked.

And Mary, steely polite, enumerated my sartorial shortcomings. But I knew one of them, at least better than she did, and I hastened to the men's room for repairs. Soap and water and a brush did wonders, but I could find no trousers, collar, or tie, and I returned clean but ragged to the box, where disapproval was being registered unanimously.

I tried to make the "prop" grin more radiant, even though I was most tired after my journey, but it didn't go with Doug and Mary.

But I refused to let them spoil my pleasure and I saw "The Three Musketeers."

It was a thrilling success for Doug. I felt good for him, though I was a bit envious. I wondered if the showing of "The Kid" could have meant as big a night for me.

'Twas quite a night, this opening of the Fairbanks masterpiece, and, considering all the circumstances, I think I behaved admirably. Somehow, though, I think there is a vote of three to one against me.

II.

OFF TO EUROPE

Next morning there was work to do. My lawyer, Nathan Burkan, had to be seen. There were contracts and other things. Almost as much a nuisance as interviews. But I dare say they are necessary.

Poor old Nath! I love him, but am afraid of him. His pockets always bulge contracts. We could be such good friends if he were not a lawyer. And I am sure that there must be times when he is delightful company. I might fire him and then get acquainted.

A very dull day with him. Interrupted by 'phones, invitations, parties, theatre tickets sent to me, people asking for jobs. Hundreds of letters camouflaged with good wishes and invariably asking favours. But I like them.

Calls from many old friends who depress me and many new ones who thrill me. I wanted some buckwheat cakes. I had to go three blocks to a Childs' restaurant to get them.

That night I went to see "Liliom," the best play in New York at the time and one which in moments rises to true greatness. It impressed me tremendously and made me dissatisfied with myself. I don't like being without work. I want to go on the stage. Wonder if I could play that part?

I went back behind the scenes and met young Skildkraut. I was amazed at his beauty and youth. Truly an artist, sincere and simple. And Eva Le Gallienne, I recall no one else on the stage just like her. She is a charming artist. We renewed our acquaintance made in Los Angeles.

The next morning provided a delightful treat. Breakfast for me, luncheon for the others, at the Coffee House Club, a most interesting little place where artists and artizans belong—writers, actors, musicians, sculptors, painters—all of them interesting people. I go there often whenever I am in New York. It was a brilliant party, Heywood Broun, Frank Crowninshield, Harrison Rhodes, Edward Knoblock, Condé Nast, Alexander Woolcott—but I can't remember all the names. I wish all meals were as pleasant.

I received an invitation to dine with Ambassador Gerard and then go for a ride in the country. The motor broke down, as they usually do on such occasions, and I had to 'phone and disappoint. I was sorry, because I was to meet some brilliant people.

I had luncheon next day with Max Eastman, one of my best friends. He is a radical and a poet and editor of *The Liberator*, a charming and sympathetic fellow who thinks. All of his doctrines I do not subscribe to, but that makes no difference in our friendship. We get together, argue a bit, and then agree to disagree and let it go at that and remain friends.

He told me of a party that he was giving at his home that evening and I hastened to accept his invitation to attend. His home is always interesting. His friends likewise.

What a night it was for me! I got out of myself. My emotions went the gamut of tears to laughter without artificiality. It was what I had left Los Angeles for, and that night Charlie Chaplin seemed very far away, and I felt or wanted to feel myself just a simple soul among other souls.

I was introduced to George, an ex-I. W. W. secretary. I suppose he has a last name, but I didn't know it and it didn't seem to matter when one met George. Here was a real personality. He had a light in his eyes that I have never seen before, a light that must have shone from his soul. He had the look of one who believes he is right and has the courage of his convictions. It is a scarce article.

I learned that he had been sentenced by Judge Landis to serve twenty year in the penitentiary, that he had served two years and was out because of ill-health. I did not learn the offence. It did not seem to matter.

A dreamer and a poet, he became wistfully gay on this hectic night among kindred spirits. In a mixed crowd of intellectuals he stood out.

He was going back to serve his eighteen years in the penitentiary and was remaining jovial. What an ordeal! But ordeal signifies what it would have been for me. I don't believe it bothered him. I hardly believe he was there. He was somewhere else in the place from which that look in his eyes emanated. A man whose ideas are ideals.

I pass no opinion, but with such charm one must sympathise.

It was an amusing evening. We played charades and I watched George act. It was all sorts of fun. We danced a bit.

Then George came in imitating Woodrow. It was screamingly funny, and he threw himself into the character, or caricature, making Wilson seem absurdly ridiculous. We were convulsed with laughter.

But all the time I couldn't help thinking that he must go back to the penitentiary for eighteen years.

What a party!

It didn't break up until two in the morning, though clock or calendar didn't get a thought from me.

We all played, danced, and acted. No one asked me to walk funny, no one asked me to twirl a cane. If I wanted to do a tragic bit, I did, and so did everyone else. You were a creature of the present, not a production of the past, not a promise of the future. You were accepted as is, *sans* "Who's Who" labels and income-tax records.

George asks me about my trip, but he does not interview. He gives me letters to friends.

In my puny way, sounding hollow and unconvincing, I try to tell George how foolish he is. He tries to explain that he can't help it. Like all trail blazers, he is a martyr. He does not rant. He blames no one. He does not rail at fate.

If he believes himself persecuted, his belief is unspoken. He is almost Christlike as he explains to me. His viewpoint is beautiful, kind, and tender.

I can't imagine what he has done to be sentenced to twenty years. My thought must speak. He believes he is spoiling my party through making me serious. He doesn't want that.

He stops talking about himself. Suddenly he runs, grabs a woman's hat, and says, "Look, Charlie, I'm Sarah Bernhardt!" and goes into a most ridiculous travesty.

I laugh. Everyone laughs. George laughs.

And he is going back to the penitentiary to spend eighteen of the most wonderful years of his life!

I can't stand it. I go out in the garden and gaze up at the stars. It is a wonderful night and a glorious moon is shining down. I wish there was something I could do for George. I wonder if he is right or wrong.

Before long George joins me. He is sad and reflective, with a sadness of beauty, not of regret. He looks at the moon, the stars. He confides, how stupid is the party, any party, compared with the loveliness of the night. The silence that is a universal gift—how few of us enjoy it. Perhaps because it cannot be bought. Rich men buy noise. Souls revel in nature's silences. They cannot be denied those who seek them.

We talk of George's future. Not of his past nor of his offence. Can't he escape? I try to make him think logically toward regaining his freedom. I want to pledge my help. He doesn't understand, or pretends not to. He has not lost anything. Bars cannot imprison his spirit.

I beg him to give himself and his life a better chance.

He smiles.

"Don't bother about me, Charlie. You have your work. Go on making the world laugh. Yours is a great task and a splendid one. Don't bother about me."

We are silent. I am choked up. I feel a sort of pent-up helplessness. I want relief. It comes.

The tears roll down my cheeks and George embraces me.

There are tears in both our eyes.

"Good-bye, Charlie."

"Good-bye, George."

What a party! Its noise disgusts me now. I call my car. I go back to the Ritz.

George goes back to the "pen."

Chuck Reisner, who played the big bully in "The Kid," called the next day. He wants to go to Europe. Why? He doesn't know. He is emotional and sensational. He is a pugilist and a song writer. A civil soldier of fortune. He doesn't like New York and thinks he wants to get back to California at once.

We have breakfast together. It is a delightful meal because it is so different from my usual lonely breakfast. Chuck goes on at a great rate and succeeds in working up his own emotions until there are tears in his eyes.

I promise him all sorts of things to get rid of him. He knows it and tells me so. We understand each other very well. I promise him an engagement. Tell him he can always get a job with me if he doesn't want too much money.

He is indignant at some press notices that have appeared about me and wants to go down to newspaper row and kill a few reporters. He fathers, mothers me in his rough way.

We talk about everybody's ingratitude for what he and I have done for people. We have a mutual-admiration convention. Why aren't we appreciated more? We are both sour on the world and its hypocrisies. It's a great little game panning the world so long as you don't let your sessions get too long or too serious.

I had a luncheon engagement at the Coffee House Club with Frank Crowninshield, and we talked over the arrangements of a dinner which I am giving to a few intimate friends. Frank is my social mentor, though I care little about society in the general acceptance of the term. We arranged for a table at the Elysée Café and it was to be a mixed party.

Among the guests were Max Eastman, Harrison Rhodes, Edward Knoblock, Mme. Maeterlinck, Alexander Woolcott, Douglas Fairbanks and Mary, Heywood Broun, Rita Weiman, and Neysa McMein, a most charming girl for whom I am posing.

Frank Harris and Waldo Frank were invited, but were unable to attend. Perhaps there were others, but I can't remember, and I am sure they will forgive me if I have neglected to mention them. I am always confused about parties and arrangements.

The last minute sets me wild. I am a very bad organiser. I am always leaving everything until the last minute, and as a rule no one shows up.

This was the exception. For on this occasion everybody did turn up. And it started off like most parties; everybody was stiff and formal; I felt a terrible failure as a host. But in spite of Mr. Volstead there was a bit of "golden water" to be had, and it saved the day. What a blessing at times!

I had been worried since sending the invitations. I wondered how Max Eastman would mix with the others, but I was soon put at my ease, because Max is clever and is just as desirous of having a good time as anyone, in spite of intellectual differences. That night he seemed the necessary ingredient to make the party.

The fizz water must have something of the sort of thing that old Ponce de Leon sought. Certainly it made us feel very young. Back to children we leaped for the night. There were games, music, dancing. And no wallflowers. Everyone participated.

We began playing charades, and Doug and Mary showed us some clever acting. They both got on top of a table and made believe he was the conductor of a trolley car and she was a passenger. After an orgy of calling out stations *en route* the conductor came along to the passenger and collected her fare. Then they both began dancing around the floor, explaining that they were a couple of fairies dancing along the side of a brook, picking flowers. Soon Mary fell in and Douglas plunged in after her and pulled her up on the banks of the brook.

That was their problem, and, guess though we would, we could not solve it.

They gave the answer finally. It was "Fairbanks."

Then we sang, and in Italian—at least it passed for that. I acted with Mme. Maeterlinck. We played a burlesque on the great dying scene of "Camille." But we gave it a touch that Dumas overlooked.

When she coughed, I got the disease immediately, and was soon taken with convulsions and died instead of Camille.

We sang some more, we danced, we got up and made impromptu speeches on any given subject. None were about the party, but on subjects like "political economy," "the fur trade," "feminism."

Each one would try to talk intelligently and seriously on a given subject for one minute. My subject was the "fur trade."

I prefaced my talk by references to cats, rabbits, etc., and finished up by diagnosing the political situation in Russia.

For me the party was a great success. I succeeded in forgetting myself for a while. I hope the rest of them managed to do the same thing. From the café the party went over to a little girl's house—she was a friend of Mr. Woolcott—and again we burst forth in music and dancing. We made a complete evening of it and I went to bed tired and exhausted about five in the morning.

I want a long sleep, but am awakened by my lawyer at nine. He has packages of legal documents and papers for me to sign, my orders about certain personal things of great importance. I have a splitting headache. My boat is sailing at noon, and altogether, with a lawyer for a companion, it is a hideous day.

All through the morning the telephone bell is ringing. Reporters. I listen several times, but it never varies.

"Mr. Chaplin, why are you going to Europe?"

"To get rid of interviews," I finally shout, and hang up the 'phone.

Somehow, with invaluable assistance, we get away from the hotel and are on our way to the dock. My lawyer meets me there. He has come to see me off. I tremble, though, for fear he has more business with me.

I am criticised by my lawyer for talking so sharply the first thing in the morning. That's just it. He always sees me the first thing in the morning. That's what makes me short.

But it is too big a moment. Something is stirring within me. I am anxious and reluctant about leaving. My emotions are all mixed.

It is a beautiful morning. New York looks much finer and nicer because I am leaving it. I am terribly troubled about passports and the usual procedure about declaring income tax, but my lawyer reassures me that he has fixed everything O.K. and that my name will work a lot of influence with the American officials; but I am very dubious about it when I am met by the American officials at the port.

I am terrified by American officials. I am extra nice to the officials, and to my amazement they are extra nice to me. Everything passes off very easily.

As usual, my lawyer was right. He had fixed everything. He is a good lawyer.

We could be such intimate friends if he wasn't.

But I am too thrilled to give much time to pitying lawyers.

I am going to Europe.

The crowds of reporters, photographers, all sorts of traffic, pushing, shoving, opening passports, visés O.K.'d, stamped, in perfect, almost clocklike precision, I am shoved aboard.

The newspaper battery pictorial and reportorial. There is no original note.

"Mr. Chaplin, why are you going to Europe?"

I feel that in this last moment I should be a bit more tolerant and pleasant, no matter how difficult. I bring forth the "prop" smile again.

"For a vacation," I answer.

Then they go through the standard interview form and I try to be obliging.

Mrs. John Carpenter is on the boat—was also invited to my party, but couldn't attend—with her charming daughter, who has the face of an angel, also Mr. Edward Knoblock. We are all photographed. Doug and Mary are there. Lots of people to see me off. Somehow I don't seem interested in them very much. My mind is pretty well occupied. I am trying to make conversation, but am more interested in the people and the boat and those who are going to travel with me.

Many of the passengers on the boat are bringing their children that I may be introduced. I don't mind children.

"I have seen you so many times in the pictures."

I find myself smiling at them graciously and pleasantly, especially the children.

I doubt if I am really sincere in this, as it is too early in the morning. Despite the fact that I love children, I find them difficult to meet. I feel rather inferior to them. Most of them have assurance, have not yet been cursed with self-consciousness.

And one has to be very much on his best behaviour with children because they detect our insincerity. I find there are quite a lot of children on board.

Everyone is so pleasant, especially those left behind. Handkerchiefs are waving. The boat is off. We start to move, the waters are churning. Am feeling very sad, rather regretful—think what a nice man my lawyer is.

We turn around the bend and get into the channel. The crowds are but little flies now. In this fleeting dramatic moment there comes the feeling of leaving something very dear behind.

The camera man and many of his brothers are aboard. I discover him as I turn around. I did not want to discover anyone just then. I wanted to be alone with sky and water. But I am still Charlie Chaplin. I must be photographed—and am.

We are passing the Statue of Liberty. He asks me to wave and throw kisses, which rather annoys me.

The thing is too obvious. It offends my sense of sincerity.

The Statue of Liberty is thrilling, dramatic, a glorious symbol. I would feel self-conscious and cheap in deliberately waving and throwing kisses at it. I will be myself.

I refuse.

The incident of the photographic seeker before the Statue of Liberty upset me. I felt that he was trying to capitalise the statue. His request was deliberate, insincere. It offended me. It would have been like calling an audience to witness the placing of flowers upon a grave. Patriotism is too deep a feeling to depict in the posing for a photograph. Why are attempts made to parade such emotions? I feel glad that I have the courage to refuse.

As I turn from the photographer I feel a sense of relief. I am to have a reprieve from such annoyances. Reporters for the while are left behind. It is a delicious sense of security.

I am ready for the new adjustment. I am in a new world, a little city of its own, where there are new people—people who may be either pleasant or unpleasant, and mine is the interesting job of placing them in their proper category. I want to explore new lands and I feel that I shall have ample opportunity on such an immense ship. The *Olympic* is enormous and I conjure up all sorts of pleasure to be had in its different rooms—Turkish baths, gymnasium, music rooms—its Ritz-Carlton restaurant, where everything is elaborate and of ornate splendour. I find myself looking forward to my evening meal.

We go to the Ritz grill to dine. Everyone is pleasant. I seem to sense the feel of England immediately. Foreign food—a change of system—the different bill of fare, with money in terms of pounds, shillings, and pence. And the dishes—pheasant, grouse, and wild duck. For the first time I feel the elegant gentleman, the man of means.

I ask questions and discover that there are really some very interesting people aboard. But I resent anyone telling me about them. I want to discover them myself. I almost shout when someone tries to read me a passenger list. This is my desert island—I am going to explore it myself. The prospect is intriguing. I am three thousand miles from Hollywood and three thousand miles from Europe. For the moment I belong to neither.

God be praised, I am myself.

It is my little moment of happiness, the glorious "to-day" that is sandwiched in between the exhausting "yesterday" of Los Angeles and the portentous "to-morrow" of Europe.

For the moment I am content.

III.

DAYS ON SHIPBOARD

I notice a thoughtful-looking, studious sort of man seated across from us. He is reading a book, a different sort of book, if covers mean anything. It looks formidable, a sort of intellectual fodder. I wonder who he is. I weave all sorts of romance about him. I place him in all sorts of intellectual undertakings, though he may be a college professor. I would love to know him. I feel that he is interested in us. I mention it to Knoblock. He keeps looking at us. Knoblock tells me he is Gillette, the safety-razor man. I feel like romancing about him more than ever. I wonder what he is reading? I would love to know him. It is our loss, I believe. And I never learned what the book was that he was reading.

There are very few pretty girls aboard. I never have any luck that way. And it is a weakness of mine. I feel that it would be awfully pleasant to cross the ocean with a number of nice girls who were pretty and who would take me as I am. We listened to the music and retired early, this because of a promise to myself that I would do lots of reading aboard. I have a copy of Max Eastman's poems, colours of life, a volume of treasures. I try to read them, but am too nervous. The type passes in parade, but I assimilate nothing, so I prepare to sleep and be in good shape for the morning. But that is also impossible.

I am beyond sleep to-night now. I am in something new, something pregnant with expectation. The immediate future is too alluring for sleep.

How shall I be received in England? What sort of a trip shall I have? Whom shall I meet on board? The thoughts chased one another round my brain and back again, all running into one another in their rambling.

I get up at one o'clock. Decide to read again. This time H. G. Wells's *Outline of History*. Impossible! It doesn't register. I try to force it by reading aloud. It can't be done. The tongue can't cheat the brain, and right now reading is out of the question.

I get up and go to see if Knoblock is in. He sleeps audibly and convincingly. He is not making his debut.

I go back to my room. I rather feel sorry for myself. If only the Turkish baths were open I could while a few hours of time away until morning. Thus I mediate. The last thing I remember it is four o'clock in the morning and the next thing eleven-thirty. I can hear a great bit of excitement going on outside my cabin door. There are a lot of little children there with autograph books. I tell them that I will sign them later and have them leave the books with my secretary, Tom Harrington.

There is a composite squeal of pleasure at this and a sickening fear comes over me. I call Tom. He enters amid a raft of autograph books. I start to sign, then postpone it until after breakfast.

Knoblock comes in all refreshed and with that radiant sort of cheerfulness that I resent in the morning. Am I going to get up for lunch or will I have it in my cabin? There is a pleading lethargy that says, "Take it in bed," but I cannot overcome the desire to explore and the feeling of expectancy of something about to happen—I was to see somebody or meet somebody—so I decide to have luncheon in the dining-room. I am giving myself the emotional stimulus. Nothing comes off. We meet nobody.

After lunch a bit of exercise. We run around the deck for a couple of miles. It brings back thoughts of the days when I ran in Marathon races. I feel rather self-conscious, however, as I am being pointed out by passengers. With each lap it gets worse. If there was only a place where I could run with nobody looking. We finally stop and lean against the rail.

All the stewards are curious. They are trying to pick me out. I notice it and pretend not to notice it. I go up into the gymnasium and look around. There is every contrivance to give joy to healthy bodies. And best of all, nobody else is there. Wonderful!

I try the weights, the rowing machine, the travelling rings, punch the bag a bit, swing some Indian clubs, and leap to the trapeze. Suddenly the place is packed. News travels quickly aboard ship. Some come for the purpose of exercising, like myself; others out of curiosity to watch me perform. I grow careless. I don't care to go through with it. I put on my coat and hat and go to my room, finding that the old once-discarded "prop" smile is useful as I make my way through the crowd.

At four o'clock we have tea. I decide that the people are interesting. I love to meet so many. Perhaps they are the same ones I hated to see come into the gym, but I feel no sense of being paradoxical. The gymnasium belongs to individuals. The tea-room suggests and invites social intercourse. Somehow there are barriers and conventionalities that one cannot break, for all the vaunted "freedom of shipboard." I feel it's a sort of awkward situation. How is it possible to meet people on the same footing? I hear of it, I read of it, but somehow I cannot meet people myself and stay myself.

I immediately shift any blame from myself and decide that the first-class passengers are all snobs. I resolve to try the second-class or the third-class. Somehow I can't meet these people. I get irritable and decide deliberately to seek the other classes of passengers and the boat crew.

Another walk around the deck. The salt air makes me feel good in spite of my mental bothers. I look over the rail and see other passengers, second or third class, and in one large group the ship's firemen and stokers. They are the night force come on deck for a breath of air between working their shifts in the hellish heat below.

They see and recognise me. To their coal-blackened faces come smiles. They shout "Hooray!" "Hello, Charlie!" Ah, I am discovered. But I tingle all over with pleasure. As those leathery faces crack into lines through the dust I sense sincerity. There is a friendly feeling. I warm to them.

There is a game of cricket going on. That's intriguing. I love cricket. Wish I could try my hand at it. Wish there was enough spontaneity about first-cabin passengers to start a game. I wish I wasn't so darn self-conscious. They must have read my thoughts. I am invited timidly, then vociferously, to play a game. Their invitation cheers me. I feel one of them. A spirit of adventure beckons. I leap over the rail and right into the midst of it.

I carry with me into the steerage just a bit of self-consciousness—there are so many trying to play upon me. I am looked upon as a celebrity, not a cricket player. But I do my part and try and we get into the game. Suddenly a motion-picture camera man bobs up from somewhere. What leeches! He snaps a picture. This gets sickening.

One of the crew has hurriedly made himself up as "Charlie Chaplin." He causes great excitement. This also impresses me. I find myself acting a part, looking surprised and interested. I am conscious of the fact that this thing has been done many times before. Then on second thought I realise it is all new to them and that they mean well, so I try to enter into the spirit of the thing. There comes a pause in the cricket game. Nobody is very much interested in it.

I find that I have been resurrected again in character and am the centre of attraction. There are calls, "What have you done with your moustache?" I look up with a grin and ready to answer anything they ask, these chaps who labour hard and must play the same way. But I see that hundreds of first-class passengers are looking down over the rail as though at a side show. This affects my pride, though I dare say I am supersensitive. I have an idea that they think I am "Charlie" performing for them. This irritates me. I throw up my hands and say, "See you to-morrow."

One of the bystanders presents himself. "Charlie, don't you remember me?" I have a vague recollection of his face, but cannot place him.

Now I have it, of course; we worked in some show together. Yes, I can actually place him. He has a negative personality. I remember that he played a small part, a chorus man or something of the sort. This brings back all sorts of reminiscences, some depressing and others interesting. I wonder what his life has been. I remember him now very plainly. He was a bad actor, poor chap. I never knew him very well even when we worked in the same company. And now he is stoking in the hold of a ship. I think I know what his emotions are and understand the reasons. I wonder whether he understands mine.

I try to be nice, even though I discover the incident is not over interesting. But I try to make it so—try harder just because he never meant a great deal before. But now it seems to take on a greater significance, the meeting with this chap, and I find myself being extra nice to him, or at least trying to be.

Darn it all, the first-class passengers are looking on again, and I will not perform for them. They arouse pride, indignation. I have decided to become very exclusive on board. That's the way to treat them.

It is five o'clock. I decide to take a Turkish bath. Ah, what a difference travelling first class after the experience in the steerage!

There is nothing like money. It does make life so easy. These thoughts come easily in the luxury of a warm bath. I feel a little more kindly disposed toward the first-cabin passengers. After all, I am an emotional cuss.

Discover that there are some very nice people on board. I get into conversation with two or three. They have the same ideas about lots of things that I have. This discovery gives me a fit of introspection and I discover that I am, indeed, a narrow-minded little pinhead.

What peculiar sights one sees in a Turkish bath. The two extremes, fat and thin, and so seldom a perfect physique. I am a discovered man—even in my nakedness. One man will insist upon showing me how to do a hand balance in the hot room. Also a somersault and a back flip. It challenges my nimbleness. Can I do them? Good heavens—no! I'm not an acrobat, I'm an actor. I am indignant.

Then he points out the value of regular exercise, outlining for my benefit a daily course for me to do aboard. I don't want any daily course and I tell him so.

"But," says he, "if you keep this up for a week you may be able to do the stunts I do."

But I can't see it even with that prospect ahead, because to save my life I can't think of any use I would have for the hand balance, somersault, or the back flip.

I meet another man who has manœuvred until he has me pinned in a corner. He shows a vital interest in Theda Bara. Do I know her? What sort of a person is she? Does she "vamp" in real life? Do I know Louise Glaum? He sort of runs to the vampish ladies. Do I know any of the old-timers? So his conversation goes depressingly on, with me answering mostly in the negative.

A scene from "Sunnyside," one of my favourite photo plays.

They must think I am very dull. Why, anyone should know the answers to the questions they figure. There are grave doubts as to whether I am Charlie Chaplin or not. I wish they would decide that I am not. I confess that I have never met Theda Bara. They return to motion pictures of my own. How do I think up my funny stunts? It is too much. Considerably against my wishes I have to retreat from the hot room. I want to get away from this terrible, strenuous experience. But retreat is not so easy.

A little rotund individual, smiling, lets me know that he has seen a number of my pictures. He says:

"I have seen you so much in 'reel' life that I wanted to talk to you in 'real' life." He laughs at this bright little sally of his and I dare say he thinks it original. The first time I heard it I choked on my milk bottle.

But I grinned. I always do. He asked what I was taking a Turkish bath for, and I told him I was afraid of acquiring a bit of a stomach. I was speaking his language. He knew the last word in taking down stomachs. He went through all the stomach-reducing routine. He rolled, he slapped, he stretched across a couch on his stomach while he breathed deeply and counted a hundred. He had several other stunts but I stopped him. He had given me enough ideas for a beginning. He got up panting, and I noticed that the most prominent thing about him was his stomach and that he had the largest stomach in the room. But he admitted that the exercise had fixed him O.K.

Eventually he glanced down at my feet. "Good heavens! I always thought you had big feet. Have you got them insured?" I can stand it no longer. I burst through the door into the cooling room and on to the slab.

At last I am where I can relax. The masseur is an Englishman and has seen most of my pictures. He talks about "Shoulder Arms." He mentions things in my pictures that I never remembered putting there. He had always thought I was a pretty muscular guy, but was sadly disappointed.

"How do you do your funny falls?" He is surprised that I am not covered with bruises. "Do I know Clara Kimball Young? Are most of the people in pictures immoral?"

I make pretences. I am asleep. I am very tired. An audience has drifted in and I hear a remark about my feet.

I am manhandled and punched and then handed on into another room.

At last I can relax. I am about to fall asleep when one of the passengers asks if I would mind signing my autograph for him. But I conquer them. Patience wins and I fall asleep to be awakened at seven o'clock and told to get out of the bath.

I dress for dinner. We go into the smoking-room. I meet the demon camera man. I do not know him, as he is dressed up like a regular person. We get into conversation. Well, hardly conversation. He talks.

"Listen, Charlie, I am very sorry, but I've been assigned to photograph you on this trip. Now we might as well get to know each other and make it easy for both of us, so the best thing to do is to let's do it fully and get it over with. Now, let's see, I'll take to-morrow and part of the next day. I want to photograph you with the third-class passengers, then the second-class, and have you shown playing games on deck. If you have your make-up and your moustache, hat, shoes, and cane, it will be all the better."

I call for help. He will have to see my personal representative, Mr. Robinson.

He says, "I won't take 'No' for an answer."

And I let him know that the only thing he isn't going to do on the trip is to photograph me. I explain that it would be a violation of contract with the First National exhibitors.

"I have been assigned to photograph you and I'm going to photograph you," he says. And then he told me of his other camera conquests, of his various experiences with politicians who did not want to be photographed.

"I had to break through the palace walls to photograph the King of England, but I got him. Also had quite a time with Foch, but I have his face in celluloid now." And he smiled as he deprecatingly looked up and down my somewhat small and slight figure.

This is the last straw. I defy him to photograph me. For from now on I have made up my mind that I am going to lock myself in my cabin—I'll fool him.

But my whole evening is spoiled. I go to bed cursing the motion-picture industry, the makers of film, and those responsible for camera men. Why did I take the trip? What is it all for? It has gotten beyond me already and it is my trip, my vacation.

It is early, and I decide to read a bit. I pick up a booklet of poems by Claude McKay, a young negro poet who is writing splendid verse of the inspired sort. Reading a few of his gems, my own annoyances seem puny and almost childish.

I read:

The Tropics of New York.

Bananas ripe and green, and ginger root,

Cocoa in pods and alligator pears,

And tangerines and mangos and grapefruit,

Fit for the highest prize at parish fairs.

See in the windows, bringing memories

Of fruit trees laden, by low-singing rills,

And dewy dawns and mystical blue skies.

In benediction over nunlike hills.

Mine eyes grow dim and I could no more gaze.

A wave of longing through my body swept,

And a hunger for the old, familiar ways;

I turned aside and bowed my head and wept.

I read again:

Lovely, dainty Spanish Needle,

With your yellow flower and white;

Dew-decked and softly sleeping;

Do you think of me to-night?

Shadowed by the spreading mango

Nodding o'er the rippling stream,

Tell me, dear plant of my childhood,

Do you of the exile dream?

Do you see me by the brook's side,

Catching grayfish 'neath the stone,

As you did the day you whispered:

"Leave the harmless dears alone?"

Do you see me in the meadow,

Coming from the woodland spring,

With a bamboo on my shoulder

And a pail slung from a string?

Do you see me, all expectant,

Lying in an orange grove,

While the swee-swees sing above me,

Waiting for my elf-eyed love?

Lovely, dainty Spanish Needle;

Source to me of sweet delight,

In your far-off sunny Southland

Do you dream of me to-night?

I am passing this along because I don't believe it is published in this country, and I feel as though I am extending a rare treat. They brought me better rest that night—a splendid sleep.

Next morning there were more autograph books and several wireless messages from intimate friends wishing me *bon voyage*. They are all very interesting.

Also there are about two hundred ship postcards. Would I mind signing them for the stewards? I am feeling very good-natured and I enjoy signing anything this morning. I pass the forenoon till lunch time.

I really feel as though I haven't met anybody. They say that barriers are lowered aboard ship, but not for me.

Ed. Knoblock and I keep very much to ourselves. But all the time I have been sort of wondering what became of the beautiful opera singer who came aboard and was photographed with me. I wonder if being photographed together constitutes an introduction? I have not seen her since the picture.

We get seats in deck chairs. Knoblock and myself. Ed. is busy reading *Economic Democracy* by some one important. I have splendid intentions of reading Wells's *Outline of History*. My intentions falter after a few paragraphs. I look at the sea, at people passing all around the ship. Every once in a while I glance at Knoblock hoping that he is overcome by his book and that he will look up, but Knoblock apparently has no such intention.

Suddenly I notice, about twenty chairs away, the beautiful singer. I don't know why I always have this peculiar embarrassment that grips me now. I am trying to make up my mind to go over and make myself known. No, such an ordeal would be too terrific. The business of making oneself known is a problem. Here she is within almost speaking distance and I am not sure whether I shall meet her or not. I glance away again. She is looking in my direction. I pretend not to see her and quickly turn my head and get into conversation with Knoblock, who thinks I have suddenly gone insane.

"Isn't that lady the opera singer?" I ask.

"Yes."

That about expresses his interest.

"Shouldn't we go over and make ourselves known?" I suggest.

"By all means, if you wish it." And he is up and off almost before I can catch my breath.

We get up and walk around the deck. I just do not know how to meet people. At last the moment comes in the smoking-room, where they are having "log auction." She is with two gentlemen. We meet. She introduces one as her husband, the other as a friend.

She reprimands me for not speaking to her sooner. I try to pretend that I had not seen her. This amuses her mightily and she becomes charming. We become fast friends. Both she and her husband join us at dinner the following night. We recall mutual friends. Discover that there are quite a lot of nice people aboard. She is Mme. Namara and in private life Mrs. Guy Bolton, wife of the author of "Sally." They are on their way to London where he is to witness the English opening of "Sally." We have a delightful evening at dinner and then later in their cabin

IV.

HELLO, ENGLAND!

Everything sails along smoothly and delightfully until the night of the concert for the seaman's fund. This entertainment is customary on all liners and usually is held on the last night out. The passengers provide the entertainment.

I am requested to perform. The thought scares me. It is a great tragedy, and, much as I would like to do something, I am too exhausted and tired. I beg to be excused, I never like making appearances in public. I find that they are always disappointing.

I give all manner of reasons for not appearing—one that I have no particular thing to do, nothing arranged for, that it is against my principles because it spoils illusion—especially for the children. When they see me minus my hat, cane, and shoes, it is like taking the whiskers off Santa Claus. And not having my equipment with me, I feel very conscious of this. I am always self-conscious when meeting children without my make-up for that very reason. I must say the officers were very sympathetic and understood my reasons for not wanting to appear, and I can assure you that the concert was a distinct success without me. There were music and recitations and singing and dancing, and one passenger did a whistling act, imitating various birds and animals, also the sawing of wood, with the screeching sound made when the saw strikes a knot. It was very effective.

I watched and enjoyed the concert immensely until near the end, when the entertainment chairman announced that I was there and that if the audience urged strongly enough I might do something for them. This was very disconcerting, and after I had explained that I was physically exhausted and had nothing prepared I am sure the audience understood. The chairman, however, announced that it did not matter, as they could see Charlie Chaplin at any time for a nickel—and that's that.

The next day is to be the last aboard. We are approaching land. I have got used to the boat and everybody has got used to me. I have ceased to be a curiosity. They have taken me at my face value—face without moustache and kindred make-up. We have exchanged addresses, cards, invitations; have made new friends, met a lot of charming people, names too numerous to mention.

The lighter is coming out. The top deck is black with men. Somebody tells me they are French and British camera men coming to welcome me. I am up on the top deck, saying good-bye to Mme. Namara and her husband. They are getting off at Cherbourg. We are staying aboard.

Suddenly there is an avalanche. All sorts and conditions of men armed with pads, pencils, motion-picture cameras, still cameras. There is an embarrassing pause. They are looking for Charlie Chaplin. Some have recognised me. I see them searching among our little group. Eventually I am pointed out.

"Why, here he is!"

My friends suddenly become frightened and desert me. I feel very much alone, the victim. Square-headed gentlemen with manners different—they are raising their hats.

"Do I speak French?" Some are speaking in French to me—it means nothing, I am bewildered. Others English. They all seem too curious to even do their own business. I find that they are personally interested. Camera men are forgetting to shoot their pictures.

But they recover themselves after their curiosity has been gratified. Then the deluge.

"Are you visiting in London?"

"Why did you come over?"

"Did you bring your make-up?"

"Are you going to make pictures over here?"

Then from Frenchmen:

"Will I visit France?"

"Am I going to Russia?"

I try to answer them all.

"Will you visit Ireland?"

"I don't expect to do so."

"What do you think of the Irish question?"

"It requires too much thought."

"Are you a Bolshevik?"

"I am an artist, not a politician."

"Why do you want to visit Russia?"

"Because I am interested in any new idea."

"What do you think of Lenin?"

"I think him a very remarkable man."

"Why?"

"Because he is expressing a new idea."

"Do you believe in Bolshevism?"

"I am not a politician?"

Others ask me to give them a message to France. A message to London. What have I to say to the people of Manchester? Will I meet Bernard Shaw? Will I meet H. G. Wells? Is it true that I am going to be knighted? How would I solve the unemployment problem?

In the midst of all this a rather mysterious gentleman pulls me to one side and tells me that he knew my father intimately and acted as agent for him in his music-hall engagements. Did I anticipate working? If so, he could get me an engagement. Would I give him the first opportunity? Anyway, he was very pleased to meet me. If I wanted a nice quiet rest I could come down to his place and spend a few days with my kind of people, the people I liked.

I am rescued by my secretaries, who insist that I go to my cabin and lie down. Anything the newspaper men have to ask they will answer for me. I am dragged away bewildered.

Is this what I came six thousand miles for? Is this rest? Where is that vacation that I pictured so vividly?

I lie down and nap until dinner time. I have dinner in my cabin. Now comes another great problem.

Tipping. One has the feeling that if you are looked at you should tip. One thing that I believe in, though—tipping. It gets you good service. It is money well spent. But when and how to tip—that is the question. It is a great problem on shipboard.

There's the bedroom steward, the waiter, the head waiter, the hallboy, the deck steward, boots, bathroom steward, Turkish bath attendants, gymnasium instructor, smoking-room steward, lounge-room steward, page boys, elevator boys, barber. It is depressing. I am harassed as to whether to tip the doctor and the captain.

I am all excited now; full of expectancy. Wonder what's going to happen. After my first encounter with fifty newspaper men at Cherbourg, somehow I do not resent it. Rather like it, in fact. Being a personage is not so bad. I am prepared for the fray. It is exciting. I am advancing on Europe. One o'clock. I am in my cabin. We are to dock in the morning.

I look out of the porthole. I hear voices. They are alongside the dock. Am very emotional now. The mystery of it out there in blackness envelops me. I revel in it—its promise. We are at Southampton. We are in England.

To-morrow! I go to bed thinking of it. To-morrow!

I try to sleep, childishly reasoning that in sleeping I will make the time pass more quickly. My reasoning was sound, perhaps, but somewhere in my anatomy there slipped a cog. I could not sleep. I rolled and tossed, counted sheep, closed my eyes and lay perfectly still, but it was no go. Somewhere within me there stirred a sort of Christmas Eve feeling. To-morrow was too portentous.

I look at my watch. It is two o'clock in the morning. I look through the porthole. It is pitch dark outside. I try to pierce the darkness, but can't. Off in the distance I hear voices coming out of the night. That and the lapping of the waves against the side of the boat.

Then I hear my name mentioned once, twice, three times. I am thrilled. I tingle with expectancy and varying emotions. It is all so peculiar and mysterious. I try to throw off the feeling. I can't.

There seems to be no one awake except a couple of men who are pacing the deck. Longshoremen, probably. Every once in a while I hear the mystic "Charlie Chaplin" mentioned. I peer through the porthole. It is starting to rain. This adds to the spell. I turn out the lights and get back to bed and try to sleep. I get up again and look out.

I call Robinson. "Can you sleep?" I ask.

"No. Let's get up and dress." It's got him, too.

We get up and walk around the top deck. There is a curious mixture of feelings all at once. I am thrilled and depressed. I cannot understand the depression. We keep walking around the deck, looking over the side. People are looking up, but they don't recognise me in the night. I feel myself speculating, wondering if it is going to be the welcome I am expecting.

Scores of messages have been arriving all day.

"Will you accept engagements?" "Will you dine with us?" "How about a few days in the country?" I cannot possibly answer them all. Not receiving replies, they send wireless messages to the captain.

"Mr. Lathom, is Mr. Chaplin on board?" "Has my message been delivered?"

I have never received so many messages. "Will you appear on Tuesday?" "Will you dine here?" "Will you join a revue?" "Are you open for engagements?" "I am the greatest agent in the world."

One of the messages is from the Mayor of Southampton, welcoming me to that city. Others from heads of the motion-picture industry in Europe. This is a source of great worriment. Welcomed by the mayor. It will probably mean a speech. I hate speeches, I can't make them. This is the worst spectre of the night.

In my sleeplessness I go back to my cabin and try to write down what I shall say, trying to anticipate what the mayor will say to me. I picture his speech of welcome. A masterpiece of oratory brought forth after much preparation by those who are always making speeches. It is their game, this speech-making, and I know I shall appear a hopeless dub with my reply.

But I attack it valiantly. I write sentence after sentence and then practise before the mirror.

"Mr. Mayor and the people of Southampton." The face that peers back at me from the mirror looks rather silly. I think of Los Angeles and wonder how they would take my speech there. But I persevere. I write more. I overcome that face in the looking-glass to such an extent that I want a wider audience.

I call Carl Robinson. I make him sit still and listen. I make my speech several times. He is kind the first time and the second time, but after that he begins to get fidgety.

He makes suggestions. I take out some lines and put in others. I decide that it is prepared and leave it. I am to meet the mayor in the morning at eight o'clock.

Eventually I get to bed and asleep, a fitful, tossing sleep. They wake me in the morning. People are outside my door. Carl comes in.

"The mayor is upstairs waiting for you." I am twenty minutes late. This adds to my inefficiency.

I am pushed and tumbled into my clothes, then taken by the arm, as if I were about to be arrested, and led from my cabin. Good Lord! I've forgotten my slip—my speech, my answer to the mayor, with its platform gestures that I had laboured with during the long night. I believed that I had created some new gestures never before attempted on platform, or in pulpit, but I was lost without my copy.

But there is little time for regrets. It doesn't take long to reach any place when that place is holding something fearful for you. I was before the mayor long before I was ready to see him.

This mayor wasn't true to type. He was more like a schoolmaster. Very pleasant and concise, with tortoiseshell rims to his glasses and with none of the ornaments of chain and plush that I had anticipated as part of the regalia of his office. This was somewhat of a relief.

There are lots of men, women and children gathered about. I am introduced to the children. I am whirled around into the crowd, and when I turn back I can't quite make out who is the mayor. There seems to be a roomful of mayors. Eventually I am dug from behind. I turn. I am whirled back by friendly or official assistance. Ah, here is the mayor.

I am welcomed by the Mayor of Southampton.

I stand bewildered, twirling my thumbs, quite at a loss as to what is expected of me.

The mayor begins. I have been warned that it is going to be very formal.

"Mr. Chaplin, on behalf of the citizens of Southampton—"

Nothing like I had anticipated. I am trying to think. Trying to hear precisely what he says. I think I have him so far. But it is nothing like I had anticipated. My speech doesn't seem to fit what he is saying. I can't help it. I will use it anyhow, at least as much as I can recall.

It is over. I mumble some inane appreciation. Nothing like I had written, with nary a gesture so laboriously rehearsed.

There comes interruptions of excited mothers with their children.

"This is my little girl."

I am shaking hands mechanically with everybody. From all sides autograph albums are being shoved under my nose. Carl is warding them off, protecting me as much as possible.

I am aware that the mayor is still standing there. I am trying to think of something more to say. All visions of language seem to have left me. I find myself mumbling. "This is nice of you" and "I am very glad to meet you all."

Somebody whispers in my ear, "Say something about the English cinema." "Say a word of welcome to the English." I try to and can't utter a word, but the same excitement that had bothered me now comes forward to my aid.

The whole thing is bewildering and thrilling and I find that I am pleased with it all.

But now strange faces seem to fade out and familiar ones take their places. There is Tom Geraghty, who used to be Doug Fairbanks'sscenario writer. He wrote "When the Clouds Roll By" and "The Mollycoddle." Tom is a great friend of mine and we have spent many a pleasant hour in Doug's home in Los Angeles. There is Donald Crisp, who played Battling Burrows in "Broken Blossoms," a clubmate in the Los Angeles Athletic Club.

My cousin, Aubrey Chaplin, a rather dignified gentleman, but with all the earmarks of a Chaplin, greets me.

Heavens! I look something like him. I picture myself in another five years. Aubrey has a saloon in quite a respectable part of London. I feel that Aubrey is a nice simple soul and quite desirous of taking me in hand.

Then Abe Breman, manager of the United Artists' affairs in England. And there is "Sonny," a friend in the days when I was on the stage. I have not heard from him in ten years. It makes me happy and interested, the thought of reviving the old friendship.

We talk of all sorts of subjects. Sonny is prosperous and doing well. He tells me everything in jerky asides, as we are hustled about amidst the baggage and bundled into a compartment that somebody has arranged.

Somehow the crowds here are not so large as I had anticipated. I am a little shocked. What if they don't turn up? Every one has tried to impress upon me the size of the reception I am to get. There is a tinge of disappointment, but then I am informed that, the boat being a day late, the crowd expected had no way of knowing when I would arrive.

This explanation relieves me tremendously, though it is not so much for myself that I feel this, but for my companions and my friends, who expect so much. I feel that the whole thing should go off with a bang for their sake. Yes, I do.

But I am in England. There is freshness. There is glow. There is Nature in its most benevolent mood. The trains, those little toy trains with the funny little wheels like those on a child's toy. There are strange noises. They come from the engine— snorting, explosive sounds, as though it was clamoring for attention.

I am in another world. Southampton, though I have been there before, is absolutely strange to me. There is nothing familiar. I feel as though I am in a foreign country. Crowds, increasing with every minute. What lovely women, different from American women. How, why, I cannot tell.

There is a beautiful girl peering at me, a lovely English type. She comes to the carriage and in a beautiful, musical voice says, "May I have your signature, Mr. Chaplin?" This is thrilling. Aren't English girls charming? She is just the type you see in pictures, something like Hall Caine's Gloria in *The Christian*—beautiful auburn hair, about seventeen.

Seventeen! What an age! I was that once—and here, in England. It seems very long ago.

Tom Geraghty and the bunch, we are all so excited we don't know just what to do or how to act. We cannot collect ourselves. Bursting with pent-up questions of years of gathering, overflowing with important messages for one another, we are talking about the most commonplace things. I find that I am not listening to them, nor they to me. I am just taking it all in, eyes and ears.

An English "bobby." Everything is different. Taking the tickets. The whole thing is upside down. The locking us in our compartment. I look at the crowds. The same old "prop" smile is working. They smile. They cheer. I wave my hat. I feel silly, but it seems that they like it. Will the train never start? I want to see something outside the station.

I want to see the country. They are all saying things. I do not know what they all think of me, my friends. I wish they were not here. I would love to be alone so that I could get it all.

We are moving. I sit forward as though to make the train go faster. I want a sight of Old England. I want more than a sight.

Now I see the English country. New houses going up everywhere. New types for labouring men. More new houses. I have never seen Old England in such a frenzy of building. The brush fields are rather burned up. This is something new for England, for it is always so green. It is not as green as it used to be. But it is England, and I am loving every mile of it.

I discover that everything is Los Angeles in my compartment, with the exception of my cousin and Sonny. Here I am in the midst of Hollywood. I have travelled six thousand miles to get away from Hollywood. Motion pictures are universal. You can't run away from them. But I am not bothering much, because I am cannily figuring on shaking the whole lot of them after the usual dinner and getting off by myself.

And I am getting new thrills every minute. There are people waiting all along the line, at small stations, waiting for the train to pass. I know they are waiting to see me. It's a wonderful sensation—everybody so affectionate. Gee! I am wondering what's going to happen in London?

Aubrey and the bunch are talking about making a strong-arm squad around me for protection. I intimately feel that it is not going to be necessary. They say: "Ah, you don't know, my boy. Wait until you get to London."

Secretly, I am hoping it is true. But I have my doubts. Everybody is nice. They suggest that I should sleep awhile, as I look tired. I feel that I am being pampered and spoiled. But I like it. And they all seem to understand.

My cousin interests me. He warns me what to talk about. At first I felt a little conscious in his presence. A little sensitive. His personality—how it mixes with my American friends. I sense that I am shocking him with my American points of view.

He has not seen me in ten years. I know that I am altered. I sort of want to pose before him a little. I want to shock him; no, not exactly shock him, but surprise him. I find myself deliberately posing and just for him. I want to be different, and I want him to know that I am a different person. This is having its effect.

Aubrey is bewildered. I am sure that he doesn't know me. I feel that I am not acting according to his schedule. It encourages me.

I become radical in my ideas. Against his conservatism. But I am beginning not to like this performing for him. One feels so conscious. I am wondering whether he will understand. There are lots of other people I have got to meet. I won't be able to devote all my time to him. I shall have a long talk with Aubrey later and explain everything. I doze off for a while.

But just for a moment. We are coming to the outskirts of London. I hear nothing, I see nothing, but I know it is so and I awake. Now I am all expectancy. We are entering the suburbs of the city.

V.

I ARRIVE IN LONDON

London! There are familiar buildings. This is thrilling. The same buildings. They have not altered. I expected that England would be altered. It isn't. It's the same. The same as I left it, in spite of the War. I see no change, not even in the manner of the people.

There's Doulton's Potteries! And look, there's the Queen's Head public-house that my cousin used to own. I point it out to him decidedly, but he reminds me that he has a much better place now. Now we are coming into the Cut. Can it be true? I can see two or three familiar stores. This train is going too fast. I want more time with these discoveries. I find my emotions almost too much for me. I have more sentiment about the buildings than I have the people.

The recognition of these localities! There is a lump rising in my throat from somewhere. It is something inexplicable. They are there, thank God!

If I could only be alone with it all. With it as it is, and with it as I would people it with ghosts of yesterday. I wish these people weren't in the compartment. I am afraid of my emotions.

The dear old Cut. We are getting into it now. Here we are. There are all conceivable kinds of noises, whistles, etc. Crowds, throngs lined up on the platforms. Here comes a police sergeant looking for a culprit. He looks straight at me. Good Lord! I am going to be arrested! But no, he smiles.

A shout, "There he is!"

Previous to this we had made resolutions. "Don't forget we are all to lock arms, Knoblock, my cousin, Robinson, Geraghty, and myself."

Immediately I get out of the train, however, we somehow get disorganised and our campaign manœuvre is lost. Policemen take me by each arm. There are motion-picture men, still-camera men. I see a sign announcing that motion pictures of my trip on board ship will be shown that night at a picture theatre. That dogged photographer of the boat must have gotten something in spite of me.

I am walking along quite the centre of things. I feel like royalty. I find I am smiling. A regular smile. I distinguish distant faces among those who crowd about me. There are voices at the end of the platform.

"Here he is. He is there, he is. That's him." My step is lightning gay. I am enjoying each moment. I am in Waterloo Station, London.

The policemen are very excited. It is going to be a terrible ordeal for them. Thousands are outside. This also thrills me. Everything is beyond my expectations. I revel in it secretly. They all stop to applaud as I come to the gate. Some of them say:

"Well done, Charlie." I wonder if they mean my present stunt between the bobbies. It is too much for me.

What have I done? I feel like a cricketer who has made a hundred and is going to the stand. There is real warm affection. Do I deserve even a part of it?

A young girl rushes out, breaks the line, makes one leap, and smothers me with a kiss. Thank God, she is pretty. There seem to be others ready to follow her, and I find myself hesitating a bit on my way. It is a signal. The barriers are broken.

They are coming on all sides. Policemen are elbowing and pushing. Girls are shrieking.

"Charlie! Charlie! There he is! Good luck to you. Charlie. God bless you." Old men, old women, girls, boys, all in one excited thrill. My friends are missing. We are fighting our way through the crowd. I do not mind it at all. I am being carried on the crest of a wave. Everybody is working but me. There seems to be no effort. I am enjoying it—lovely.

Eventually we get through to the street. It is worse here. "Hooray!" "Here he is!" "Good luck, Charlie!" "Well done, Charlie!" "God bless you. God love you!" "Good luck, Charlie!" Bells are ringing. Handkerchiefs are waving. Some are raising their hats. I have lost mine. I am bewildered, at a loss, wondering where it is all leading to, but I don't care. I love to stay in it.

Suddenly there is a terrific crash. Various currents of the crowd are battling against one another. I find that now I am concerned about my friends. Where's Tom? Where's So-and-so? Where's Carl? Where's my cousin? I'm asking it all aloud, on all sides, of anyone who will listen to me. I am answered with smiles.

I am being pushed toward an automobile.

"Where's my cousin?" Another push.

Policemen on all sides. I am pushed and lifted and almost dumped into the limousine. My hat is thrown in behind me. There are three policemen on each side of the car, standing on the running board. I can't get out. They are telling the chauffeur to drive on. He seems to be driving right over the people. Occasionally a head, a smiling face, a hand, a hat flashes by the door of the car. I ask and keep asking, "Where's my cousin?"

But I regain myself, straighten my clothes, cool off a bit, and look round. There is a perfect stranger in the limousine with me. I seem to take him for granted for the moment. He is also cut up and bleeding. Evidently he is somebody. He must be on the schedule to do something. He looks bewildered and confused.

I say, "Well—I have missed my cousin."

He says, "I beg your pardon, I have not been introduced to you."

"Do you know where we are going?" I ask.

He says, "No."

"Well, what are you doing—Who are you?" I splutter.

"No one in particular," he answers. "I have been pushed in here against my will. I think it was the second time you cried for your cousin. One of the cops picked me, but I don't believe there is any relationship."

We laugh. That helps. We pull up and he is politely let off at the corner. As quickly as possible he is shut out. Crowds are around on both sides, raising their hats English fashion, as though they were meeting a lady. The mounted policemen leave us. I am left alone with my thoughts.

If I could only do something—solve the unemployment problem or make some grand gesture—in answer to all this. I look through the window in the back of the car. There are a string of taxis following behind. In the lead, seated on top of the cab, is a young and pretty girl all dressed in scarlet. She is waving to me as she chases. What a picture she makes! I think what good fun it would be to get on top of the cab with her and race around through the country.

I feel like doing something big. What an opportunity for a politician to say something and do something big! I never felt such affection. We are going down York Road. I see placards, "Charlie Arrives." Crowds standing on the corner, all lined up along my way to the hotel. I am beginning to wonder what it's all about.

Am feeling a bit reflective, after all, thinking over what I have done; it has not been very much. Nothing to call forth all this. "Shoulder Arms" was pretty good, perhaps, but all this clamour over a moving-picture actor!

Now we are passing over Westminster Bridge. There are double-decked street cars. There's one marked "Kennington."

I want to get out and get on it—I want to go to Kennington. The bridge is so small; I always thought it was much wider. We are held up by traffic. The driver tells the bobby that Charlie Chaplin is inside. There is a change in the expression of the cop.

"On your way."

By this time the policemen have dropped off the side of the car and are on their way back. Once more I am a private citizen. I am just a bit sad at this. Being a celebrity has its nice points.

There is an auto with a motion-picture camera on top of it photographing our car. I tell the driver to put down the top. Why didn't we do this before? I wanted to let the people see. It seemed a shame to hide in this way. I wanted to be seen. There are little crowds on the street corners again.

Ah yes, and Big Ben. It looks so small now. It was so big before I went away. We are turning up the Haymarket. People are looking and waving from their windows. I wave back. Crowded streets. We are nearing the Ritz, where I am to stop.

The crowds are much denser here. I am at a loss. I don't know what to do, what to say. I stand up. I wave and bow at them, smile at them, and go through the motions of shaking hands, using my own hands. Should I say something? Can I say anything? I feel the genuineness of it all, a real warmth. It is very touching. This is almost too much for me. I am afraid I am going to make a scene.

I stand up. The crowd comes to a hush. It is attentive. They see I am about to say something. I am surprised at my own voice. I can hear it. It is quite clear and distinct, saying something about its being a great moment, etc. But tame and stupid as it is, they like it.

There is a "Hooray!" "Good boy, Charlie!"

Now the problem is how am I going to get out of this? The police are there, pushing and shoving people aside to make way, but they are out-numbered. There are motion-picture cameras, cameras on the steps. The crowds close in. Then I step out. They close in. I am still smiling. I try to think of something useful, learned from my experience at the New York opening of "The Three Musketeers." But I am not much help to my comrades.

Then as we approach, the tide comes in toward the gates of the hotel. They have been kept locked to prevent the crowd from demolishing the building. I can see one intrepid motion-picture camera man at the door as the crowd starts to swarm. He begins to edge in, and starts grinding his camera frantically as he is lifted into the whirlpool of humanity. But he keeps turning, and his camera and himself are gradually turned up to the sky, and his lens is registering nothing but clouds as he goes down turning—the most honorable fall a camera man can have, to go down grinding. I wonder if he really got any pictures.

In some way my body has been pushed, carried, lifted, and projected into the hotel. I can assure you that through no action of mine was this accomplished. I am immediately introduced to some English nobleman. The air is electric. I feel now I am free. Everybody is smiling. Everybody is interested. I am shown to a suite of rooms.

I like the hotel lobby. It is grand. I am raced to my room. There are bouquets of flowers from two or three English friends whom I had forgotten. There come cards. I want to welcome them all. Do not mind in the least. Am out for the whole day of it. The crowds are outside. The manager presents himself. Everything has been spread to make my stay as happy as possible.

The crowd outside is cheering. What is the thing to do? I had better go to the window. I raise my hands again. I pantomime, shake hands with myself, throw them kisses. I see a bouquet of roses in the room. I grab it and start tossing the flowers into the crowd. There is a mad scramble for the souvenirs. In a moment the chief of police bursts into my room.

"Please, Mr. Chaplin, it is very fine, but don't throw anything. You will cause an accident. They will be crushed and killed. Anything but that, don't throw anything. If you don't mind, kindly refrain from throwing anything." Excitedly he repeats his message over and over again.

Of course I don't mind; the flowers are all gone, anyway. But I am theatrically concerned. "Ah, really I am so sorry. Has anything happened?" I feel that everything is all right.

The rest of my friends arrive all bruised and cut up. Now that the excitement has died down, what are we going to do? For no reason at all we order a meal. Nobody is hungry. I want to get out again. Wish I could.

I feel that everybody ought to leave immediately. I want to be alone. I want to get out and escape from all crowds. I want to get over London, over to Kennington, all by myself. I want to see some familiar sights. Here baskets of fruit keep pouring in, fresh bouquets, presents, trays full of cards, some of them titles, some well-known names—all paying their respects. Now I am muddled. I don't know what to do first. There is too much waiting. I have too much of a choice.

But I must get over to Kennington, and to-day. I am nervous, overstrung, tense. Crowds are still outside. I must go again and bow and wave my hands. I am used to it, am doing it mechanically; it has no effect. Lunch is ordered for everybody. Newspaper men are outside, visitors are outside. I tell Carl to get them to put it off until to-morrow. He tells them that I am tired, need a rest, for them to call to-morrow and they will be given an interview.

The bishop of something presents his compliments. He is in the room when I arrive. I can't hear what he is saying. I said 'yes, I shall be delighted.' We sit down to lunch. What a crowd there is eating with me! I am not quite sure I know them all.

Everyone is making plans for me. This irritates me. My cousin, Tom Geraghty, Knoblock—would I spend two or three days in the country and get a rest? No. I don't want to rest. Will you see somebody? I don't want to see anybody. I want to be left entirely alone. I've just got to have my whim.

I make a pretence at lunch. I whisper to Carl, "You explain everything to them—tell them that I am going out immediately after lunch." I am merely taking the lunch to discipline myself.

I look out the window. The crowds are still there. What a problem! How am I going to get out without being recognised? Shall I openly suggest going out, so I can get away? I hate disappointing them. But I must go out.

Tom Geraghty, Donald Crisp, and myself suggest taking a walk. I do not tell them my plans, merely suggest taking the walk. We go through the back way and escape. I am sure that everything is all right, and that no one will recognise me. I cannot stand the strain any longer. I tell Donald and Tom—they really must leave me alone. I want to be alone, and want to visit alone. They understand. Tom is a good sort and so is Donald. I do not want to ride, but just for a quicker means of getting away I call a taxicab.

I tell him to drive to Lambeth. He is a good driver, and an old one. He has not recognised me, thank heaven!

But he is going too fast. I tell him to drive slower, to take his time. I sit back now. I am passing Westminster Bridge again. I see it better. Things are more familiar. On the other side is the new London County Council building. They have been building it for years. They started it before I left.

The Westminster Road has become very dilapidated, but perhaps it is because I am riding in an automobile. I used to travel across it another way. It doesn't seem so long ago, either.

My God! Look! Under the bridge! There's the old blind man. I stop the driver and drive back. We pull up outside the Canterbury.

"You wait there, or do you want me to pay you off?" He will wait. I walk back.

There he is, the same old figure, the same old blind man I used to see as a child of five, with the same old earmuffs, with his back against the wall and the same stream of greasy water trickling down the stone behind his back.

The same old clothes, a bit greener with age, and the irregular bush of whiskers coloured almost in a rainbow array, but with a dirty grey predominant.

What a symbol from which to count the years that I had been away. A little more green to his clothes! A bit more grey in his matted beard!

He has that same stark look in his eyes that used to make me sick as a child. Everything exactly the same, only a bit more dilapidated.

No. There is a change. The dirty little mat for the unhealthy-looking pup with the watering eyes that used to be with him—that is gone. I would like to hear the story of the missing pup.

Did its passing make much difference to the lonely derelict? Was its ending a tragic one, dramatic, or had it just passed out naturally?

The old man is laboriously reading the same chapter from his old, greasy, and bethumbed embossed Bible. His lips move, but silently, as his fingers travel over the letters. I wonder if he gets comfort there? Or does he need comfort?

To me it is all too horrible. He is the personification of poverty at its worst, sunk in that inertia that comes of lost hope. It is too terrible.

VI.

THE HAUNTS OF MY CHILDHOOD

I jump into the automobile again and we drive along past Christ Church. There's Baxter Hall, where we used to see magic-lantern slides for a penny. The forerunner of the movie of to-day. I see significance in everything around me. You could get a cup of coffee and a piece of cake there and see the Crucifixion of Christ all at the same time.

We are passing the police station. A drear place to youth. Kennington Road is more intimate. It has grown beautiful in its decay. There is something fascinating about it.

Sleepy people seem to be living in the streets more than they used to when I played there. Kennington Baths, the reason for many a day's hookey. You could go swimming there, second class, for three pence (if you brought your own swimming trunks).

Through Brook Street to the upper Bohemian quarter, where third-rate music-hall artists appear. All the same, a little more decayed, perhaps. And yet it is not just the same.

I am seeing it through other eyes. Age trying to look back through the eyes of youth. A common pursuit, though a futile one.

It is bringing home to me that I am a different person. It takes the form of art; it is beautiful. I am very impersonal about it. It is another world, and yet in it I recognise something, as though in a dream.

We pass the Kennington "pub," Kennington Cross, Chester Street, where I used to sleep. The same, but, like its brother landmarks, a bit more dilapidated. There is the old tub outside the stables where I used to wash. The same old tub, a little more twisted.

I tell the driver to pull up again. "Wait a moment." I do not know why, but I want to get out and walk. An automobile has no place in this setting. I have no particular place to go. I just walk along down Chester Street. Children are playing, lovely children. I see myself among them back there in the past. I wonder if any of them will come back some day and look around enviously at other children.

Somehow they seem different from those children with whom I used to play. Sweeter, more dainty were these little, begrimed kids with their arms entwined around one another's waists. Others, little girls mostly, sitting on the doorsteps, with dolls, with sewing, all playing at that universal game of "mothers."

For some reason I feel choking up. As I pass they look up. Frankly and without embarrassment they look at the stranger with their beautiful, kindly eyes. They smile at me. I smile back. Oh, if I could only do something for them. These waifs with scarcely any chance at all.

Now a woman passes with a can of beer. With a white skirt hanging down, trailing at the back. She treads on it. There, she has done it again. I want to shriek with laughter at the joy of being in this same old familiar Kennington. I love it.

It is all so soft, so musical; there is so much affection in the voices. They seem to talk from their souls. There are the inflections that carry meanings, even if words were not understood. I think of Americans and myself. Our speech is hard, monotonous, except where excitement makes it more noisy.

There is a barber shop where I used to be the lather boy. I wonder if the same old barber is still there? I look. No, he is gone. I see two or three kiddies playing on the porch. Foolish, I give them something. It creates attention. I am about to be discovered.

I leap into the taxi again and ride on. We drive around until I have escaped from the neighbourhood where suspicion has been planted and come to the beginning of Lambeth Walk. I get out and walk along among the crowds.

People are shopping. How lovely the cockneys are! How romantic the figures, how sad, how fascinating! Their lovely eyes. How patient they are! Nothing conscious about them. No affectation, just themselves, their beautifully gay selves, serene in their limitations, perfect in their type.

I am the wrong note in this picture that nature has concentrated here. My clothes are a bit conspicuous in this setting, no matter how unobtrusive my thoughts and actions. Dressed as I am, one never strolls along Lambeth Walk.

I feel the attention I am attracting. I put my handkerchief to my face. People are looking at me, at first slyly, then insistently. Who am I? For a moment I am caught unawares.

A girl comes up—thin, narrow-chested, but with an eagerness in her eyes that lifts her above any physical defects.

"Charlie, don't you know me?"

Of course I know her. She is all excited, out of breath. I can almost feel her heart thumping with emotion as her narrow chest heaves with her hurried breathing. Her face is ghastly white, a girl about twenty-eight. She has a little girl with her.

This girl was a little servant girl who used to wait on us at the cheap lodging-house where I lived. I remembered that she had left in disgrace. There was tragedy in it. But I could detect a certain savage gloriousness in her. She was carrying on with all odds against her. Hers is the supreme battle of our age. May she and all others of her kind meet a kindly fate.

With pent-up feelings we talk about the most commonplace things.

"Well, how are you, Charlie?"

"Fine." I point to the little girl. "Is she your little girl?"

She says, "Yes."

That's all, but there doesn't seem to be much need of conversation. We just look and smile at each other and we both weave the other's story hurriedly through our own minds by way of the heart. Perhaps in our weaving we miss a detail or two, but substantially we are right. There is warmth in the renewed acquaintance. I feel that in this moment I know her better than I ever did in the many months I used to see her in the old days. And right now I feel that she is worth knowing.

There's a crowd gathering. It's come. I am discovered, with no chance for escape. I give the girl some money to buy something for the child, and hurry on my way. She understands and smiles. Crowds are following. I am discovered in Lambeth Walk.

But they are so charming about it. I walk along and they keep behind at an almost standard distance. I can feel rather than hear their shuffling footsteps as they follow along, getting no closer, losing no ground. It reminds me of the Pied Piper of Hamelin.

All these people just about five yards away, all timid, thrilled, excited at hearing my name, but not having the courage to shout it under this spell.

"There he is." "That's 'im." All in whispers hoarse with excitement and carrying for great distance, but at the same time repressed by the effort of whispering. What manners these cockneys have! The crowds accumulate. I am getting very much concerned. Sooner or later they are going to come up, and I am alone, defenceless. What folly this going out alone, and along Lambeth Walk!

Eventually I see a bobby, a sergeant—or, rather, I think him one, he looks so immaculate in his uniform. I go to him for protection.

"Do you mind?" I say. "I find I have been discovered. I am Charlie Chaplin. Would you mind seeing me to a taxi?"

"That's all right, Charlie. These people won't hurt you. They are the best people in the world. I have been with them for fifteen years." He speaks with a conviction that makes me feel silly and deservedly rebuked.

I say, "I know it; they are perfectly charming."

"That's just it," he answers. "They are charming and nice."

They had hesitated to break in upon my solitude, but now, sensing that I have protection, they speak out.

"Hello, Charlie!" "God bless you, Charlie!" "Good luck to you, lad!" As each flings his or her greetings they smile and self-consciously back away into the group, bringing others to the fore for their greeting. All of them have a word—old women, men, children. I am almost overcome with the sincerity of their welcome.

We are moving along and come to a street corner and into Kennington Road again. The crowds continue following as though I were their leader, with nobody daring to approach within a certain radius.

The little cockney children circle around me to get a view from all sides.

I see myself among them. I, too, had followed celebrities in my time in Kennington. I, too, had pushed, edged, and fought my way to the front rank of crowds, led by curiosity. They are in rags, the same rags, only more ragged.

They are looking into my face and smiling, showing their blackened teeth. Good God! English children's teeth are terrible! Something can and should be done about it. But their eyes!

Soulful eyes with such a wonderful expression. I see a young girl glance slyly at her beau. What a beautiful look she gives him! I find myself wondering if he is worthy, if he realises the treasure that is his. What a lovely people!

We are waiting. The policeman is busy hailing a taxi. I just stand there self-conscious. Nobody asks any questions. They are content to look. Their steadfast watching is so impressing. I feel small—like a cheat. Their worship does not belong to me. God, if I could only do something for all of them!

But there are too many—too many. Good impulses so often die before this "too many."

I am in the taxi.

"Good-bye, Charlie! God bless you!" I am on my way.

The taxi is going up Kennington Road along Kennington Park. Kennington Park. How depressing Kennington Park is! How depressing to me are all parks! The loneliness of them. One never goes to a park unless one is lonesome. And lonesomeness is sad. The symbol of sadness, that's a park.

But I am fascinated now with it. I am lonesome and want to be. I want to commune with myself and the years that are gone. The years that were passed in the shadow of this same Kennington Park. I want to sit on its benches again in spite of their treacherous bleakness, in spite of the drabness.

But I am in a taxi. And taxis move fast. The park is out of sight. Its alluring spell is dismissed with its passing. I did not sit on the bench. We are driving toward Kennington Gate.

Kennington Gate. That has its memories. Sad, sweet, rapidly recurring memories.

'Twas here, my first appointment with Hetty (Sonny's sister). How I was dolled up in my little, tight-fitting frock coat, hat, and cane! I was quite the dude as I watched every street car until four o'clock waiting for Hetty to step off, smiling as she saw me waiting.

I get out and stand there for a few moments at Kennington Gate. My taxi driver thinks I am mad. But I am forgetting taxi drivers. I am seeing a lad of nineteen, dressed to the pink, with fluttering heart, waiting, waiting for the moment of the day when he and happiness walked along the road. The road is so alluring now. It beckons for another walk, and as I hear a street car approaching I turn eagerly, for the moment almost expecting to see the same trim Hetty step off, smiling.

The car stops. A couple of men get off. An old woman. Some children. But no Hetty.

Hetty is gone. So is the lad with the frock coat and cane.

Back into the cab, we drive up Brixton Road. We pass Glenshore Mansions—a more prosperous neighbourhood. Glenshore Mansions, which meant a step upward to me, where I had my Turkish carpets and my red lights in the beginning of my prosperity.

We pull up at The Horns for a drink. The same Horns. Used to adjoin the saloon bar. It has changed. Its arrangement is different. I do not recognise the keeper. I feel very much the foreigner now; do not know what to order. I am out of place. There's a barmaid.

How strange, this lady with the coiffured hair and neat little shirtwaist!

"What can I do for you, sir?"

I am swept off my feet. Impressed. I want to feel very much the foreigner. I find myself acting.

"What have you got?"

She looks surprised.

"Ah, give me ginger beer." I find myself becoming a little bit affected. I refuse to understand The money—the shillings and the pence. It is thoroughly explained to me as each piece is counted before me. I go over each one separately and then leave it all on the table.

There are two women seated at a near-by table. One is whispering to the other. I am recognised.

"That's 'im; I tell you 'tis."

"Ah, get out! And wot would 'e be a-doin' 'ere?"

I pretend not to hear, not to notice. But it is too ominous. Suddenly a white funk comes over me and I rush out and into the taxi again. It's closing time for a part of the afternoon. Something different. I am surprised. It makes me think it is Sunday. Then I learn that it is a new rule in effect since the war.

I am driving down Kennington Road again. Passing Kennington Cross.

Kennington Cross.

It was here that I first discovered music, or where I first learned its rare beauty, a beauty that has gladdened and haunted me from that moment. It all happened one night while I was there, about midnight. I recall the whole thing so distinctly.

I was just a boy, and its beauty was like some sweet mystery. I did not understand. I only knew I loved it and I became reverent as the sounds carried themselves through my brain *via* my heart.

I suddenly became aware of a harmonica and a clarinet playing a weird, harmonious message. I learned later that it was "The Honeysuckle and the Bee." It was played with such feeling that I became conscious for the first time of what melody really was. My first awakening to music.

I remembered how thrilled I was as the sweet sounds pealed into the night. I learned the words the next day. How I would love to hear it now, that same tune, that same way!

Conscious of it, yet defiant, I find myself singing the refrain softly to myself:

You are the honey, honeysuckle. I am the bee;

I'd like to sip the honey, dear, from those red lips. You see

I love you dearie, dearie, and I want you to love me—

You are my honey, honeysuckle. I am your bee.

Kennington Cross, where music first entered my soul. Trivial, perhaps, but it was the first time.

There are a few stragglers left as I pass on my way along Manchester Bridge at the Prince Road. They are still watching me. I feel that Kennington Road is alive to the fact that I am in it. I am hoping that they are feeling that I have come back, not that I am a stranger in the public eye.

I am on my way back. Crossing Westminster Bridge. I enter a new land. I go back to the Haymarket, back to the Ritz to dress for dinner.

VII.

A JOKE AND STILL ON THE GO

In the evening I dined at the Ritz with Ed. Knoblock, Miss Forrest, and several other friends. The party was a very congenial one and the dinner excellent. It did much to lift me from the depression into which the afternoon in Kennington had put me.

Following dinner we said "Good night" to Miss Forrest, and the rest of us went around to Ed. Knoblock's apartment in the Albany. The Albany is the most interesting building I have yet visited in London.

In a sort of dignified grandeur it stands swathed in an atmosphere of tradition. It breathes the past, and such a past! It has housed men like Shelley and Edmund Burke and others whose fame is linked closely with the march of English civilisation.

Naturally, the building is very old. Ed.'s apartment commands a wonderful view of London. It is beautifully and artistically furnished, its high ceilings, its tapestries, and its old Victorian windows giving it a quaintness rather startling in this modern age.

We had a bit of supper, and about eleven-thirty it began to rain, and later there was a considerable thunderstorm.

Conversation, languishing on general topics, turns to me, the what and wherefore of my coming and going, my impressions, plans, etc. I tell them as best I can.

Knoblock is anxious to get my views on England, on the impression that London has made. We discuss the matter and make comparisons. I feel that England has acquired a sadness, something that is tragic and at the same time beautiful.

We discuss my arrival. How wonderful it was. The crowds, the reception. Knoblock thinks that it is the apex of my career. I am inclined to agree with him.

Whereupon Tom Geraghty comes forward with a startling thought. Tom suggests that I die immediately. He insists that this is the only fitting thing to do, that to live after such a reception and ovation would be an anti-climax. The artistic thing to do would be to finish off my career with a spectacular death. Everyone is shocked at his suggestion. But I agree with Tom that it would be a great climax. We are all becoming very sentimental; we insist to one another that we must not think such thoughts, and the like.

The lightning is flashing fitfully outside. Knoblock, with an inspiration, gathers all of us, except Tom Geraghty, into a corner and suggests that on the next flash of lightning, just for a joke, I pretend to be struck dead, to see what effect it would have on Tom.

We make elaborate plans rapidly. Each is assigned to his part in the impromptu tragedy. We give Tom another drink and start to talking about death and kindred things. Then we all comment how the wind is shaking this old building, how its windows rattle and the weird effect that lightning has on its old tapestries and lonely candlesticks. Surreptitiously, some one has turned out all but one light, but old Tom does not suspect.

The atmosphere is perfect for our hoax and several of us who are "in the know" feel sort of creepy as we wait for the next flash. I prime myself for the bit of acting.

The flash comes, and with it I let forth a horrible shriek, then stand up, stiffen, and fall flat on my face. I think I did it rather well, and I am not sure but that others beside Tom were frightened.

Tom drops his whisky glass and exclaims: "My God! It's happened!" and his voice is sober. But no one pays any attention to him.

They all rush to me and I am carried feet first into the bedroom, and the door closed on poor old Tom, who is trying to follow me in. Tom just paces the floor, waiting for some one to come from the bedroom and tell him what has happened. He knocks on the door several times, but no one will let him in.

My "property grin."

Finally, Carl Robinson comes out of the room, looking seriously intent, and Tom rushes to him.

"For God's sake, Carl, what's wrong?"

Carl brushes him aside and makes for the telephone.

"Is he—dead?" Tom puts the question huskily and fearfully.

Carl pays no attention except: "Please don't bother me now, Tom. This is too serious." Then he calls on the telephone for the coroner. This has such an effect on Geraghty that Knoblock comes forth from the bedroom to pacify him.

"I am sure it will be all right," Knoblock says to Tom, at the same time looking as though he were trying to keep something secret. Everything is staged perfectly and poor old Tom just stands and looks bewildered, and every few moments tries to break into the bedroom, but is told to stay out, that he is in no condition to be mixing up in anything so serious.

The chief of police is called, doctors are urged to rush there in all haste with motors, and with each call Tom's suffering increases. We keep up the joke until it has reached the point of artistry, and then I enter from the bedroom in a flowing sheet for a gown and a pillow slip on each arm to represent wings, and I proceed to be an angel for a moment.

But the effect has been too great on Tom, and even the travesty at the finish does not get a laugh from him.

We laughed and talked about the stunt for a while and Tom was asked what he would have done if it had been true and I had been hit by the lightning

Tom made me feel very cheap and sorry that I had played the trick on him when he said that he would have jumped out of the window himself, as he would have no desire to live if I were dead.

But we soon got away from serious things and ended the party merrily and went home about five in the morning. Which meant that we would sleep very late that day.

Three o'clock in the afternoon found me awakened by the news that there was a delegation of reporters waiting to see me. They were all ushered in and the whole thirty-five of them started firing questions at me in a bunch. And I answered them all, for by this time I was quite proficient with reporters, and as they all asked the same questions that I had answered before it was not hard.

In fact, we all had luncheon or tea together, though for me it was breakfast, and I enjoyed them immensely. They are real, sincere, and intelligent and not hero worshippers.

Along about five o'clock Ed. Knoblock came in with the suggestion that we go out for a ride together and call around to see Bernard Shaw. This did sound like a real treat. Knoblock knows Shaw very well and he felt sure that Shaw and I would like each other.

First, though, I propose that we take a ride about London, and Ed. leads the way to some very interesting spots, the spots that the tourist rarely sees as he races his way through the buildings listed in guide books

He takes me to the back of the Strand Theatre, where there are beautiful gardens and courts suggesting palaces and armour and the days when knights were bold. These houses were the homes of private people during the reign of King Charles and even farther back. They abound in secret passages and tunnels leading up to the royal palace. There is an air about them that is aped and copied, but it is not hard to distinguish the real from the imitation. History is written on every stone; not the history of the battlefield that is laid bare for the historians, but that more intimate history, that of the drawing-room, where, after all, the real ashes of empires are sifted.

Now we are in Adelphi Terrace, where Bernard Shaw and Sir James Barrie live. What a lovely place the terrace is! And its arches underneath leading to the river. And at this hour, six-thirty, there comes the first fall of evening and London with its soft light is at its best.

I can quite understand why Whistler was so crazy about it. Its lighting is perfect—so beautiful and soft. Perhaps there are those who complain that it is poorly lighted and who would install many modern torches of electricity to remedy the defect, but give me London as it is. Do not paint the lily.

We make for Shaw's house, which overlooks the Thames Embankment. As we approach I feel that this is a momentous occasion. I am to meet Shaw. We reach the house. I notice on the door a little brass name plate with the inscription, "Bernard Shaw." I wonder if there is anything significant about Shaw's name being engraved in brass. The thought pleases me. But we are here, and Knoblock is about to lift the knocker.

And then I seem to remember reading somewhere about dozens of movie actors going abroad, and how they invariably visited Shaw. Good Lord! the man must be weary of them. And why should he be singled out and imposed upon? And I do not desire to ape others. And I want to be individual and different. And I want Bernard Shaw to like me. And I don't want to force myself upon him.

And all this is occurring very rapidly, and I am getting fussed, and we are almost before him, and I say to Knoblock, "No, I don't want to meet him."

Ed. is annoyed and surprised and thinks I am crazy and everything. He asks why, and I suddenly become embarrassed and shy. "Some other time," I beg. "We won't call to-day." I don't know why, but suddenly I feel self-conscious and silly—

Would I care to see Barrie? He lives just across the road.

"No, I don't want to see any of them to-day." I am too tired. I find that it would be too much effort.

So I go home, after drinking in all the beauties of the evening, the twilight, and the loveliness of Adelphi Terrace. This requires no effort. I can just drift along on my own, let thoughts come and go as they will, and never have to think about being polite and wondering if I am holding my own in intelligent discussion that is sure to arise when one meets great minds. I wasted the evening just then. Some other time, I know, I am going to want Shaw and Barrie.

I drift along with the sight and am carried back a hundred years, two hundred, a thousand. I seem to see the ghosts of King Charles and others of Old England with the tombstones epitaphed in Old English and dating back even to the eleventh century.

It is all fragrant and too fleeting. We must get back to the hotel to dress for dinner.

Then Knoblock, Sonny, Geraghty, and a few others dine with me at the Embassy Club, but Knoblock, who is tired, leaves after dinner. Along about ten o'clock Sonny, Geraghty, Donald Crist, Carl Robinson, and myself decide to take a ride. We make toward Lambeth. I want to show them Lambeth. I feel as if it is mine—a choice discovery and possession that I wish to display.

I recall an old photographer's shop in the Westminster Bridge Road just before you come to the bridge. I want to see it again. We get out there. I remember having seen a picture framed in that window when I was a boy—a picture of Dan Leno, who was an idol of mine in those days.

The picture was still there, so is the photographer—the name "Sharp" is still on the shop. I tell my friends that I had my picture taken here about fifteen years ago, and we went inside to see if we could get one of the photos.

"My name is Chaplin," I told the person behind the counter. "You photographed me fifteen years ago. I want to buy some copies."

"Oh, we destroyed the negative long ago," the person behind the counter thus dismisses me.

"Have you destroyed Mr. Leno's negative?" I ask him.

"No," was the reply, "but Mr. Leno is a famous comedian."

Such is fame. Here I had been patting myself on the back, thinking I was some pumpkins as a comedian, and my negative destroyed. However, there is balm in Gilead. I tell him I am Charlie Chaplin and he wants to turn the place upside down to get some new pictures of me; but we haven't the time, and, besides, I want to get out, because I am hearing suppressed snickers from my friends, before whom I was going to show off.

VIII.

A MEMORABLE NIGHT IN LONDON

So we wandered along through South London by Kennington Cross and Kennington Gate, Newington Butts, Lambeth Walk, and the Clapham Road, and all through the neighbourhood. Almost every step brought back memories, most of them of a tender sort. I was right here in the midst of my youth, but somehow I seemed apart from it. I felt as though I was viewing it under a glass. It could be seen all too plainly, but when I reached to touch it it was not there—only the glass could be felt, this glass that had been glazed by the years since I left.

If I could only get through the glass and touch the real live thing that had called me back to London. But I couldn't.

A man cannot go back. He thinks he can, but other things have happened to his life. He has new ideas, new friends, new attachments. He doesn't belong to his past, except that the past has, perhaps, made marks on him.

My friends and I continue our stroll—a stroll so pregnant with interest to me at times that I forget that I have company and wander along alone.

Who is that old derelict there against the cart? Another landmark. I look at him closely. He is the same—only more so. Well do I remember him, the old tomato man. I was about twelve when I first saw him, and he is still here in the same old spot, plying the same old trade, while I—

I can picture him as he first appeared to me standing beside his round cart heaped with tomatoes, his greasy clothes shiny in their unkemptness, the rather glassy single eye that had looked from one side of his face staring at nothing in particular, but giving you the feeling that it was seeing all, the bottled nose with the network of veins spelling dissipation.

I remember how I used to stand around and wait for him to shout his wares. His method never varied. There was a sudden twitching convulsion, and he leaned to one side, trying to straighten out the other as he did so, and then, taking into his one good lung all the air it would stand, he would let forth a clattering, gargling, asthmatic, high-pitched wheeze, a series of sounds which defied interpretation.

Somewhere in the explosion there could be detected "ripe tomatoes." Any other part of his message was lost.

And he was still here. Through summer suns and winter snows he had stood and was standing. Only a bit more decrepit, a bit older, more dyspeptic, his clothes greasier, his shoulder rounder, his one eye rather filmy and not so all-seeing as it once was. And I waited. But he did not shout his wares any more. Even the good lung was failing. He just stood there inert in his ageing. And somehow the tomatoes did not look so good as they once were.

We get into a cab and drive back towards Brixton to the Elephant and Castle, where we pull up at a coffee store. The same old London coffee store, with its bad coffee and tea.

There are a few pink-cheeked roués around and a couple of old derelicts. Then there are a lot of painted ladies, many of them with young men and the rest of them looking for young men. Some of the young fellows are minus arms and many of them carry various ribbons of military honour. They are living and eloquent evidence of the War and its effects. There are a number of stragglers. The whole scene to me is depressing. What a sad London this is! People with tired, worn faces after four years of War!

Someone suggests that we go up and see George Fitzmaurice, who lives in Park Lane. There we can get a drink and then go to bed. We jump in a cab and are soon there. What a difference! Park Lane is another world after the Elephant and Castle. Here are the homes of the millionaires and the prosperous.

Fitzmaurice is quite a successful moving-picture director. We find a lot of friends at his house, and over whiskies-and-sodas we discuss our trip. Our trip through Kennington suggests Limehouse, and conversation turns toward that district and Thomas Burke.

I get their impressions of Limehouse. It is not as tough as it has been pictured. I rather lost my temper through the discussion.

One of those in the party, an actor, spoke very sneeringly of that romantic district and its people.

"Talk about Limehouse nights. I thought they were tough down there. Why, they are like a lot of larks!" said this big-muscled leading man.

And then he tells of a visit to the Limehouse district—a visit made solely for the purpose of finding trouble. How he had read of the tough characters there and how he had decided to go down to find out how tough they were.

"I went right down there into their joints," he said, "and told them that I was looking for somebody that was tough, the tougher the better, and I went up to a big mandarin wearing a feather and said: 'Give me the toughest you've got. You fellows are supposed to be tough down here, so let's see how tough you are.' And I couldn't get a rise out of any of them," he concluded.

This was enough for me. It annoyed.

I told him that it was very fine for well-fed, over-paid actors flaunting toughness at these deprived people, who are gentle and nice and, if ever tough, only so because of environment. I asked him just how tough he would be if he were living the life that some of these unfortunate families must live. How easy for him, with five meals a day beneath that thrust-out chest with his muscles trained and perfect, trying to start something with these people. Of course they were not tough, but when it comes to four years of War, when it comes to losing an arm or a leg, then they are tough. But they are not going around looking for fights unless there is a reason.

It rather broke up the party, but I was feeling so disgusted that I did not care.

We meander along, walking from Park Lane to the Ritz.

On our way we are stopped by two or three young girls. They are stamped plainly and there is no subtlety about their "Hello boys! You are not going home so early?" They salute us. We wait a moment. They pause and then wave their hands to us and we beckon them.

"How is it you are up so late?" They are plainly embarrassed at this question. Perhaps it has been a long time since they were given the benefit of the doubt. They are not sure just what to say. We are different. Their usual method of attack or caress does not seem in order, so they just giggle.

Here is life in its elemental rawness. I feel very kindly disposed toward them, particularly after my bout with the well-fed actor who got his entertainment from the frailties of others. But it is rather hard for us to mix. There is a rather awkward silence.

Then one of the girls asks if we have a cigarette. Robinson gives them a package, which they share between the three of them. This breaks the ice. They feel easier. The meeting is beginning to run along the parliamentary rules that they know.

Do we know where they can get a drink?

"No." This is a temporary setback, but they ask if we mind their walking along a bit with us. We don't, and we walk along towards the Ritz. They are giggling, and before long I am recognised. They are embarrassed.

They look down at their shabby little feet where ill-fitting shoes run over at the heels. Their cheap little cotton suits class them even low in their profession, though their youth is a big factor toward their potential rise when they have become hardened and their mental faculties have become sharpened in their eternal battles with men. Then men will come to them.

Knowing my identity, they are on their good behaviour. No longer are we prospects. We are true adventure for them this night. Their intimacy has left them and in its place there appears a reserve which is attractive even in its awkwardness.

The conversation becomes somewhat formal. And we are nearing the hotel, where we must leave them. They are very nice and charming now, and are as timid and reserved as though they had just left a convent.

They talk haltingly of the pictures they have seen, shyly telling how they loved me in "Shoulder Arms," while one of them told how she wept when she saw "The Kid" and how she had that night sent some money home to a little kid brother who was in school and staying there through her efforts in London.

The difference in them seems so marked when they call me Mr. Chaplin and I recall how they had hailed us as "Hello, boys." Somehow I rather resent the change. I wish they would be more intimate in their conversation. I would like to get their viewpoint. I want to talk to them freely. They are so much more interesting than most of the people I meet.

But there is a barrier. Their reserve stays. I told them that I was sure they were tired and gave them cab fare.

One of their number speaks for the trio.

"Thanks, Mr. Chaplin, very much. I could do with this, really. I was broke, honest. Really, this comes in very handy."

They could not quite understand our being nice and sympathetic.

They were used to being treated in the jocular way of street comradery. Finer qualities came forward under the respectful attention we gave them, something rather nice that had been buried beneath the veneer of their trade.

Their thanks are profuse, yet awkward. They are not used to giving thanks. They usually pay, and pay dearly, for anything handed them. We bid them "good night." They smile and walk away.

We watch them for a bit as they go on their way. At first they are strolling along, chattering about their adventure. Then, as if on a signal, they straighten up as though bracing themselves, and with quickened steps they move toward Piccadilly, where a haze of light is reflected against the murky sky.

It is the beacon light from their battleground, and as we follow them with our eyes these butterflies of the night make for the lights where there is laughter and gaiety.

As we go along to the Ritz we are all sobered by the encounter with the three little girls. I think blessed is the ignorance that enables them to go on without the mental torture that would come from knowing the inevitable that awaits them.

As we go up the steps of the hotel we see a number of derelicts huddled asleep against the outside of the building, sitting under the arches and doors, men and women, old and young, underfed, deprived, helpless, so much so that the imprint of helplessness is woven into their brain and brings on an unconsciousness that is a blessing.

We wake them up and hand them each money. "Here, get yourself a bed."

They are too numbed. They thank us mechanically, accepting what we give them, but their reaction and thanks are more physical than mentahere was one old woman about seventy. I gave her something. She woke up, or stirred in her sleep, took the money without a word of thanks—took it as though it was her ration from the bread line and no thanks were expected, huddled herself up in a tighter knot than before, and continued her slumber. The inertia of poverty had long since claimed her.

We rang the night bell at the Ritz, for they are not like our American hotels, where guests are in the habit of coming in at all hours of the night. The Ritz closes its doors at midnight, and after that hour you must ring them.

But the night was not quite over. As we were ringing the bell we noticed a waggon a little way off in the street, with the horse slipping and the driver out behind the waggon with his shoulder to the wheel and urging the horse along with cheery words.

We walked to the waggon and found it was loaded with apples and on its way to the market. The streets were so slippery that the horse could not negotiate the hill. I could not help but think how different from the usual driver this man was.

He did not belay the tired animal with a whip and curse and swear at him in his helplessness. He saw that the animal was up against it, and instead of beating him he got out and put his shoulder to the wheel, never for the moment doubting that the horse was doing his best.

We all went out into the street and put our shoulders against the waggon along with the driver. He thanked us, and as we finally got the momentum necessary to carry it over the hill he said:

"These darn roads are so slippery that the darned horse even can't pull it."

It was a source of wonder to him that he should come upon something too much for his horse. And the horse was so well fed and well kept. I could not help but notice how much better the animal looked than his master. The evening was over. I don't know but that the incident of the apple waggon was a fitting finale.

The next morning for the first time I am made to give my attention to the mail that has been arriving. We have been obliged to have another room added to our suite in order to have some place in which to keep the numerous sacks that are being brought to us at all hours.

The pile is becoming so mountainous that we are compelled to engage half a dozen stenographers just for the purpose of reading and classifying them.

We found that there were 73,000 letters or cards addressed to me during the first three days in London, and of this number more than 28,000 were begging letters—letters begging anywhere from £1 to £100,000.

Countless and varied were the reasons set forth. Some were ridiculous. Some were amusing. Some were pathetic. Some were insulting. All of them in earnest

I discovered from the mail that there are relatives of mine in England that I knew nothing about.

The greater part of these were cousins, and they gave very detailed family-tree tracings in support of their claims. All of them wished to be set up in business or to get into the movies.

But the cousins did not have a monopoly on the relationships. There were brothers and sisters and aunts and uncles, and there were nine claiming to be my mother, telling wondrous adventure stories about my being stolen by gipsies when a baby or being left on doorsteps, until I began to think my youth had been a very hectic affair. But I did not worry much about these last, as I had left a perfectly good mother back in California, and so far I have been pretty much satisfied with her.

There were letters addressed just to Charles Chaplin, some to King Charles, some to the "King of Mirth"; on some there was drawn the picture of a battered derby; some carried a reproduction of my shoes and cane; and in some there was stuck a white feather with the question as to what I was doing during the war?

Would I visit such and such institutions? Would I appear for such and such charity? Would I kick off the football season or attend some particular Soccer game? Then there were letters of welcome and one enclosing an iron cross inscribed, "For your services in the Great War," and "Where were you when England was fighting?"

Then there were others thanking me for happiness given the senders. These came by the thousand. One young soldier sent me four medals he had gotten during the big war. He said that he was sending them because I had never been properly recognised. His part was so small and mine so big, he said, that he wanted me to have his *Croix de Guerre*, his regimental and other medals.

Some of the letters were most interesting. Here are a few samples:

Dear Mr. Chaplin,—You are a leader in your line and I am a leader in mine. Your speciality is moving pictures and custard pies. My speciality is windmills.

I know more about windmills than any man in the world. I have studied the winds all over the world and am now in a position to invent a windmill that will be the standard mill of the world, and it will be made so it can be adapted to the winds of the tropics and the winds of the arctic regions.

I am going to let you in on this in an advantageous way. You have only to furnish the money. I have the brains, and in a few years I will make you rich and famous. You had better 'phone me for quick action.

Dear Mr. Chaplin,—Won't you please let me have enough money to send little Oscar to college? Little Oscar is twelve, and the neighbours all say that he is the brightest little boy they have ever seen. And he can imitate you so well that we don't have to go to the movies any more. [This is dangerous. Oscar is a real competitor, ruining my business.] And so, if you can't send the little fellow to college, won't you take him in the movies with you like you did Jackie Coogan?

Dear Mr. Chaplin,—My brother is a sailor, and he is the only man in the world who knows where Capt. Kidd's gold is buried. He has charts and maps and everything necessary, including a pick and shovel. But he cannot pay for the boat.

Will you pay for the boat, and half the gold is yours? All you need do is to say "yes" to me in a letter, and I will go out and look for John as he is off somewhere on a bust, being what you might call a drinking man when ashore. But I am sure that I can find him, as he and I drink in the same places. Your shipmate.

Dear Charlie,—Have you ever thought of the money to be made in peanuts? I know the peanut industry, but I am not telling any of my business in a letter. If you are interested in becoming a peanut king, then I'm your man. Just address me as Snapper Dodge, above address.

Dear Mr. Chaplin,—My daughter has been helping me about my boarding-house now for several years, and I may say that she understands the art of catering to the public as wishes to stay in quarters. But she has such high-toned ideas, like as putting up curtains in the bathroom and such that at times I think she is too good for the boarding-house business and should be having her own hotel to run.

If you could see your way to buy a hotel in London or New York for Drusilla, I am sure that before long your name and Drusilla's would be linked together all over the world because of what Drusilla would do to the hotel business. And she would save money because she could make all the beds and cook herself, and at nights could invent the touches like what I have mentioned. Drusilla is waiting for you to call her.

Dear Mr. Chaplin,—I am enclosing pawn tickets for Grandma's false teeth and our silver water pitcher, also a rent bill showing that our rent was due yesterday. Of course, we would rather have you pay our rent first, but if you could spare it, grandma's teeth would be acceptable, and we can't hold our heads up among the neighbours since father sneaked our silver pitcher to get some beer.

IX.

I MEET THE IMMORTALS

Here are extracts from a number of letters selected at random from the mountain of mail awaiting me at the hotel:

"—— wishes Mr. Chaplin a hearty welcome and begs him to give him the honour of shaving him on Sunday, Sept. any time which he thinks suitable."

A West End moneylender has forwarded his business card, which states: "Should you require temporary cash accommodation, I am prepared to advance you £ to £10,000 on note of hand alone, without fees or delay. All communications strictly private and confidential."

A man living in Golden Square, W., writes: "My son, in the endeavour to get a flower thrown by you from the Ritz Hotel, lost his hat, the bill for which I enclose, seven shillings and sixpence."

A Liverpool scalp specialist gathers that Mr. Chaplin is much concerned regarding the appearance of grey hairs in his head. "I claim to be," he adds, "the only man in Great Britain who can and does restore the colour of grey hair. You may visit Liverpool, and if you will call I shall be pleased to examine your scalp and give you a candid opinion. If nothing can be done I will state so frankly."

"Is there any chance," writes a woman of Brixton, "of you requiring for your films the services of twin small boys nearly four years old and nearly indistinguishable? An American agent has recently been in this neighbourhood and secured a contract with two such small girls (twins), which points to at least a demand for such on American films."

A widow of sixty-two writes: "I have a half-dozen china teaset of the late Queen Victoria's diamond jubilee, and it occurred to me that you might like to possess it. If you would call or allow me to take it anywhere for you to see, I would gladly do so. I have had it twenty-four years, and would like to raise money on it."

A South London picture dealer writes: "If ever you should be passing this way when you are taking your quiet strolls around London, I would like you to drop in and see a picture that I think might interest you. It is the Strand by night, painted by Arthur Grimshaw in 1887. I hope you won't think I have taken too much of a liberty—but I knew your mother when I was in Kate Paradise's troupe, and I think she would remember me if ever you were to mention Clara Symonds of that troupe. It is a little link with the past."

"Dear Old Friend,—Some months ago I wrote to you, and no doubt you will remember me.I was in 'Casey's Court,' and, as you know, we had Mr. Murray for our boss. You have indeed got on well. I myself have only this month come home from being in Turkey for eight years. Dear old boy, I should like to see you when you come to London—that is, if you do not mind mixing with one of the Casey's Court urchins."

A Sussex mother writes: "Would you grant a few moments' interview to a little girl of nine (small for her years) whom I am anxious to start on the films? She has much in her favour, being not only bright and clever, but unusually attractive in appearance, receiving unlimited attention wherever she goes, as she is really quite out of the ordinary."

A disengaged actress writes: "If you should take a film in England it would be a great kindness to employ some of the hundreds of actresses out of work now and with no prospects of getting any. A walk-on would be a very welcome change to many of us, to say nothing of a part."

A Somerset man writes: "A friend of mine has a very old-time spot right here in Somerset, with the peacocks wandering across the well-kept grounds and three lovely trout ponds, where last night I brought home five very fine rainbow trout each weighing about one-and-a-half pounds. You will be tired of the crowds. Slip away down to me and I will give you ten days or more of the best time you can get. There will be no side or style, and your oldest clothes will be the thing."

Another correspondent says: "My husband and I should consider it an honour if during your visit to South London you would call and take a homely cup of tea with us. I read in the paper of your intention to stay at an old-fashioned inn, and should like to recommend the White Horse Inn at Sheen, which, I believe, is the oldest in Surrey. It certainly corresponds with your ideal. Welcome to your home town."

This from the seaside: "When you are really tired of the rush of London there is a very nice little place called Seaford, not very far from London, just a small place where you can have a real rest. No dressing up, etc., and then fishing, golf, and tennis if you care for the same. You could put up at an hotel or here. There will be no one to worry you. Don't forget to drop us a line."

A London clubman, in offering hospitality, says: "I do not know you. You do not know me, and probably don't want to. But just think it over and come and have a bit of lunch with me one day. This between ourselves—no publicity."

"Saint Pancras Municipal Officers' Swimming Club would be greatly honoured by your presiding at our annual swimming gala to be held at the St. Pancras Public Baths."

Dorothy, writing from Poplar, asks: "Dear Mr. Charlie Chaplin, if you have a pair of old boots at home will you throw them at me for luck?"

An aspirant for the position of secretary writes: "I am a musical comedy artist by profession, but am at present out of work. I am six feet two inches in height and years of age. If there is any capacity in which you can use my services I shall be very thankful. Hoping you will have an enjoyable stay in your home country."

A Barnes man writes: "If you have time we should be very proud if you could spare an afternoon to come to tea. We should love to give you a real old-fashioned Scotch tea, if you would care to come. We know you will be fêted, and everyone will want you, but if you feel tired and want a wee rest come out quietly to us. If it wasn't for your dear funny ways on the screen during the war we would all have gone under."

"Dear Charles," writes an eleven-year-old, "I'd like to meet you very, very much. I'd like to meet you just to say thank you for all the times you've cheered me up when I've felt down and miserable. I've never met you and I don't suppose I ever will, but you will always be my friend and helper. I'd love your photograph signed by you! Are you likely to come to Harrogate? I wish you would. Perhaps you could come and see me. Couldn't you try?"

I wish I could read them all, for in every one there is human feeling, and I wish it were possible that I could accept some of the invitations, especially those inviting me to quietness and solitude. But there are thousands too many. Most of them will have to be answered by my secretaries, but all of them will be answered, and we are taking trunkfuls of the letters back to California in order that as many of the requests as possible shall receive attention.

During the afternoon there came Donald Crisp, Tom Geraghty and the bunch, and before long my apartment in the London Ritz might just as well be home in Los Angeles. I realise that I am getting nowhere, meeting nobody and still playing in Hollywood.

I have travelled 6,000 miles and find I have not shaken the dust of Hollywood from my shoes. I resent this. I tell Knoblock I must meet other people besides Geraghty and the Hollywood bunch. I have seen as much as I want to see of it. Now I want to meet people.

Knoblock smiles, but he is too kind to remind me of my retreat before the name plate of Bernard Shaw. He and I go shopping and I am measured for some clothes; then to lunch with E. V. Lucas.

Lucas is a very charming man, sympathetic and sincere. He has written a number of very good books. It is arranged to give me a party that night at the Garrick Club.

After luncheon we visit Stoll's Theatre, where "Shoulder Arms" and Mary Pickford's picture "Suds," are being shown. This is my first experience in an English cinema. The opera house is one that was built by Steinhouse and then turned into a movie theatre.

It is strange and odd to see the English audience drinking tea and eating pastry while watching the performance. I find very little difference in their appreciation of the picture. All the points tell just the same as in America. I get out without being recognised and am very thankful for that.

Another scene from "Sunnyside," one of my favourite photo plays.

Back to the hotel and rest for the evening before my dinner at the Garrick Club.

The thought of dining at the Garrick Club brought up before me the mental picture that I have always carried of that famous old meeting place in London, where Art is most dignified. And the club itself realised my picture to the fullest.

Tradition and custom are so deep-rooted there that I believe its routine would go on through sheer mechanics of spirit, even if its various employees should forget to show up some day. The corners seem almost peopled with the ghosts of Henry Irving and his comrades. There in one end of the gloomy old room is a chair in which David Garrick himself sat.

All those at the dinner were well known in art circles—E. V. Lucas, Walter Hackett, George Frampton, J. M. Barrie, Herbert Hammil, Edward Knoblock, Harry Graham, N. Nicholas, Nicholas D. Davies, Squire Bancroft, and a number of others whose names I do not remember.

What an interesting character is Squire Bancroft. I am told that he is England's oldest living actor, and he is now retired. He does not look as though he should retire.

I am late and that adds to an embarrassment which started as soon as I knew I was to meet Barrie and so many other famous people.

There is Barrie. He is pointed out to me just about the time I recognise him myself. This is my primary reason for coming. To meet Barrie. He is a small man, with a dark moustache and a deeply marked, sad face, with heavily shadowed eyes; but I detect lines of humour lurking around his mouth. Cynical? Not exactly.

I catch his eye and make motions for us to sit together, and then find that the party had been planned that way anyhow. There is the inevitable hush for introductions. How I hate it. Names are the bane of my existence. Personalities, that's the thing.

But everyone seems jovial except Barrie. His eyes look sad and tired. But he brightens as though all along there had been that hidden smile behind the mask. I wonder if they are all friendly toward me, or if I am just the curiosity of the moment.

There is an embarrassing pause, after we have filed into the dining-room, which E. V. Lucas breaks.

"Gentlemen, be seated."

I felt almost like a minstrel man and the guests took their seats as simultaneously as though rehearsed for it.

I feel very uncomfortable mentally. I cough. What shall I say to Barrie? Why hadn't I given it some thought? I am aware that Squire Bancroft is seated at my other side. I feel as though I am in a vice with its jaws closing as the clock ticks. Why did I come? The atmosphere is so heavy, yet I am sure they feel most hospitable toward me.

I steal a glance at Squire Bancroft. He looks every bit the eminent old-school actor. The dignity and tradition of the English stage is written into every line in his face. I remember Nicholson having said that the squire would not go to a "movie," that he regarded his stand as a principle. Then why is he here? He is going to be difficult, I fear.

He breaks the ice with the announcement that he had been to a movie that day! Coming from him it was almost a shock.

"Mr. Chaplin, the reading of the letter in 'Shoulder Arms' was the high spot of the picture." This serious consideration from the man who would not go to the movies.

I wanted to hug him. Then I learn that he had told everyone not to say anything about his not having been to a movie for fear that it would offend me. He leans over and whispers his age and tells me he is the oldest member of the club. He doesn't look within ten years of his age. I find myself muttering inanities in answering him.

Then Barrie tells me that he is looking for some one to play Peter Pan and says he wants me to play it. He bowls me over completely. To think that I was avoiding and afraid to meet such a man! But I am afraid to discuss it with him seriously, am on my guard because he may decide that I know nothing about it and change his mind.

Just imagine, Barrie has asked me to play Peter Pan! It is too big and grand to risk spoiling it by some chance witless observation, so I change the subject and let this golden opportunity pass. I have failed completely in my first skirmish with Barrie.

There are laboured jokes going the rounds of the table and everyone seems to feel conscious of some duty that is resting on his shoulders ungracefully.

One ruddy gentleman whose occupation is a most serious one, I am told, that of building a giant memorial in Whitehall to the dead of the late War, is reacting to the situation most flippantly. His conversation, which has risen to a pitch of almost hysterical volume, is most ridiculously comic. He is a delightful buffoon.

Everyone is laughing at his chatter, but nothing seems to be penetrating my stupidity, though I am carrying with me a wide mechanical grin, which I broaden and narrow with the nuances of the table laughing. I feel utterly out of the picture, that I don't belong, that there must be something significant in the badinage that is bandied about the board.

Barrie is speaking again about moving pictures. I must understand. I summon all of my scattered faculties to bear upon what he is saying. What a peculiarly shaped head he has.

He is speaking of "The Kid," and I feel that he is trying to flatter me. But how he does it! He is criticising the picture.

He is very severe. He declares that the "heaven" scene was entirely unnecessary, and why did I give it so much attention? And why so much of the mother in the picture, and why the meeting of the mother and the father? All of these things he is discussing analytically and profoundly, so much so that I find that my feeling of self-consciousness is rapidly leaving me.

I find myself giving my side of the argument without hesitation, because I am not so sure that Barrie is right, and I had reasons, good reasons, for wanting all those things in the picture. But I am thrilled at his interest and appreciation and it is borne in upon me that by discussing dramatic construction with me he is paying a very gracious and subtle compliment. It is sweet of him. It relieves me of the last vestige of my embarrassment.

"But, Sir James," I am saying, "I cannot agree with you—" Imagine the metamorphosis. And our discussion continues easily and pleasantly. I am aware of his age as he talks and I get more of his spirit of whimsicality.

The food is being served and I find that E. V. Lucas has provided a treacle pudding, a particular weakness of mine, to which I do justice. I am wondering if Barrie resents age, he who is so youthful in spirit.

There seems to be lots of fun in the general buffoonery that is going on around the table, but despite all efforts to the contrary I am serving a diet of silence. I feel very colourless, that the whole conversation that is being shouted is colourless.

I am a good audience. I laugh at anything and dare not speak. Why can't I be witty? Are they trying to draw me out? Maybe I am wrong and there is a purpose behind this buffoonery. But I hardly know whether to retaliate in kind, or just grin.

I am dying for something to happen. Lucas is rising. We all feel the tension. Why are parties like that? It ends.

Barrie is whispering, "Let's go to my apartment for a drink and a quiet talk," and I begin to feel that things are most worth while. Knoblock and I walk with him to Adelphi Terrace, where his apartment overlooks the Thames Embankment.

Somehow this apartment seems just like him, but I cannot convey the resemblance in a description of it. The first thing you see is a writing desk in a huge room beautifully furnished, and with dark-wood panelling. Simplicity and comfort are written everywhere. There is a large Dutch fireplace in the right side of the room, but the outstanding piece of furniture is a tiny kitchen stove in one corner. It is polished to such a point that it takes the aspect of the ornamental rather than the useful. He explains that on this he makes his tea when servants are away. Such a touch, perhaps, just the touch to suggest Barrie.

Our talk drifts to the movies and Barrie tells me of the plans for filming "Peter Pan." We are on very friendly ground in this discussion and I find myself giving Barrie ideas for plays while he is giving me ideas for movies, many of them suggestions that I can use in comedies.

There is a knock at the door. Gerald du Maurier is calling. He is one of England's greatest actors and the son of the man who wrote "Trilby." Our party lasts far into the night, until about three in the morning. I notice that Barrie looks rather tired and worn, so we leave, walking with Du Maurier up the Strand. He tells us that Barrie is not himself since his nephew was drowned, that he has aged considerably.

We walk slowly back to the hotel and to bed.

Next day there is a card from Bruce Bairnsfather, England's famous cartoonist, whose work during the war brought him international success, inviting me to tea. He carries me out into the country, where I have a lovely time. His wife tells me that he is just a bundle of nerves and that he never knows when to stop working. I ask what H. G. Wells is like and Bruce tells me that he is like "Wells" and no one else.

When I get back to the hotel there is a letter from Wells.

"Do come over. I've just discovered that you are in town. Do you want to meet Shaw? He is really very charming out of the limelight. I suppose you are overwhelmed with invitations, but if there is a chance to get hold of you for a talk, I will be charmed. How about a week-end with me at Easton, free from publicity and with harmless, human people. No 'phones in the house."

I lost no time in accepting such an invitation.

There is a big luncheon party on among my friends and I am told that a party has been arranged to go through the Limehouse district with Thomas Burke, who wrote "Limehouse Nights." I resent it exceedingly and refuse to go with a crowd to meet Burke. I revolt against the constant crowding. I hate crowds.

London and its experiences are telling on me and I am nervous and unstrung. I must see Burke and go with him alone. He is the one man who sees London through the same kind of glasses as myself.

I am told that Burke will be disappointing because he is so silent, but I do not believe that I will be disappointed in him.

Robinson tells the crowd of my feelings and how much I have planned on this night alone with Burke, and the party is called off. We 'phone Burke and I make an engagement to meet him at his home that evening at ten o'clock. We are to spend the night together in Limehouse. What a prospect!

That night I was at Thomas Burke's ahead of time. The prospect of a night spent in the Limehouse district with the author of "Limehouse Nights" was as alluring as Christmas morning to a child.

Burke is so different from what I expected. "Limehouse Nights" had led me to look for some one physically, as well as mentally, big, though I had always pictured him as mild-mannered and tremendously human and sympathetic.

I notice even as we are introduced that Burke looks tired and it is hard to think that this little man with the thin, peaked face and sensitive features is the same one who has blazed into literature such elemental lusts, passions and emotions as characterise his short stories.

I am told that he doesn't give out much. I wonder just who he is like. He is very curious. Doesn't seem to be noticing anything that goes on about him. He just sits with his arm to his face, leaning on his hand and gazing into the fire. As he sits there, apparently unperturbed and indifferent, I am warming up to him considerably. I feel a sort of master of the situation. It's a comfortable feeling. Is the reticence real or is this some wonderful trick of his, this making his guest feel superior?

His tired-looking, sensitive eyes at first seem rather severe and serious, but suddenly I am aware of something keen, quick and twinkling in them. His wife has arrived. A very young lady of great charm, who makes you feel instantly her artistic capabilities even in ordinary conversation.

Shortly after his wife comes in Burke and I leave, I feeling very much the tourist in the hands of the super city guide.

"What, where—anything particular that I want to see?"

This rather scares me, but I take it as a challenge and make up my mind that I will know him. He is difficult, and, somehow, I don't believe that he cares for movie actors. Maybe I am only possible "copy" to him?

He seems to be doing me a kindness and I find myself feeling rather stiff and on my best behaviour, but I resolve that before the evening is through I will make him open up and like me, for I am sure that his interest is well worth while.

I have nothing to suggest except that we ramble along with nothing deliberate in view. I feel that this pleases him, for a light of interest comes into his eyes, chasing one of responsibility. We are just going to stroll along.

X.

I MEET THOMAS BURKE AND H. G. WELLS

As Burke and I ramble along toward no place in particular, I talk about his book. I have read "Limehouse Nights" as he wrote it. There is nothing I could see half so effective. We discuss the fact that realities such as he has kept alive seldom happen in a stroll, but I am satisfied. I don't want to see. It could not be more beautiful than the book. There is no reaction to my flattery. I must watch good taste. I feel that he is very intelligent, and I am silent for quite a while as we stroll toward Stepney. There is a greenish mist hanging about everything and we seem to be in a labyrinth of narrow alleyways, now turning into streets and then merging into squares. He is silent and we merely walk.

And then I awaken. I see his purpose. I can do my own story—he is merely lending me the tools, and what tools they are! I feel that I have served an ample apprenticeship in their use, through merely reading his stories. I am fortified.

It is so easy now. He has given me the stories before. Now he is telling them over in pictures. The very shadows take on life and romance. The skulking, strutting, mincing, hurrying forms that pass us and fade out into the night are now becoming characters. The curtain has risen on "Limehouse Nights," dramatised with the original cast.

There is a tang of the east in the air and I am tinglingly aware of something vital, living, moving, in this murky atmosphere that is more intense even for the occasional dim light that peers out into the soft gloom from attic windows and storerooms, or municipal lights that gleam on the street corners.

Here is a little slice of God's fashioning, where love runs hand in hand with death, where poetry sings in withered Mongolian hearts, even as knives are buried in snow-white breasts and swarthy necks. Here hearts are broken casually, but at the same time there comes just as often to this lotus land the pity, terror, and wonder of first love, and who shall say which is predominant?

Behind each of those tiny garret windows lurks life—life in its most elemental costume. There is no time, thought, or preparation for anything but the elemental passions, and songs of joy, hope, and laughter are written into each existence, even as the killings go on, surely, swiftly.

There must be a magic wand forever doing a pendulum swing over this land, for the point of view often changes from the beastly to the beautiful, and in one short moment the innocent frequently gather the sophistication of the aged. These creatures of life's game run blithely along their course ignorant of the past, joyful in the present, and careless of the future, while their tiny lightened windows seem to wink deliberately as they make pinpricks of light through the shuttered gloom.

On the other side of the street there is stepping a little lady whose cheap cotton clothes are cut with Parisian cunning, and as we cross and pass her we discern beauty, enhanced manyfold by youth and vitality, but hardened with premature knowledge. I can't help but think of little Gracie Goodnight, the little lady who resented the touch of a "Chink," so much so that she filled the fire extinguishers in his place with oil, and when he was trapped in the blazing building, calmly, and with a baby smile upon her face, poured the contents of the extinguisher over him and his furniture.

There is the Queen's Theatre, bringing forward a mental picture of little Gina of Chinatown, who stopped a panic in the fire-frightened audience of the playhouse as her début offering on the stage. Little Gina, who brought the whole neighbourhood to her feet in her joyous dancing delight. Little Gina, who at fourteen had lived, laughed, and loved, and who met death with a smile, carrying the secret of him with her.

Every once in a while Burke merely lifts his stick and points. His gesture needs no comment. He has located and made clear without language the only one object he could possibly mean, and, strangely, it is always something particularly interesting to me. He is most unusual.

What a guide he is! He is not showing me Main Street, not the obvious, not even the sightseer's landmarks, but in this rambling I am getting the heart, the soul, the feeling. I feel that he has gauged me quickly—that he knows I love feelings rather than details, that he is unconsciously flattering to my subtlety, after two miles through black, though lovely, shadows.

Now he is picking the spots where lights are shining from the fish shops. He knows their locations, knows their lights because he has studied them well. There are forms slinking gracefully, as though on location and with rehearsed movement. What an effect for a camera!

This is rugged. Here are the robust of the slums. People act more quickly here than in Lambeth. And suddenly we are back where we started. In a car we go to the old Britannia, Hoxton, rather reluctantly.

There is a glaring moving-picture palace. What a pity! I resent its obtrusion. We go along toward the East India Docks—to Shadwell. And I am feeling creepy with the horror of his stories of Shadwell. I could hear a child screaming behind a shuttered window and I wondered and imagined, but we did not stop anywhere.

We meandered along with just an occasional gesture from him, all that was necessary to make his point. To Stanhope Road, Bethnal Green, Spitalfields, Ratcliffe, Soho, Notting Dale, and Camden Town.

And through it all I have the feeling that things trivial, portentous, beautiful, sordid, cringing, glorious, simple, epochal, hateful, lovable are happening behind closed doors. I people all those shacks with girls, boys, murders, shrieks, life, beauty.

As we go back we talk of life in the world outside this adventurous Utopia. He tells me that he has never been outside of London, not even to Paris. This is very curious to me, but it doesn't seem so as he says it. He tells me of another book that he has ready and of a play that he is working on for early production. We talked until three in the morning and I went back to my hotel with the same sort of feelings that I had at twelve when I sat up all night reading Stevenson's "Treasure Island."

The next day I did some shopping, and was measured for boots. How different is shopping here! A graceful ceremony that is pleasing even to a man. The sole advertisement I see in the shop is "Patronised by His Majesty." It is all said in that one phrase.

And the same methods have been in vogue at this bootmaker's for centuries. My foot is placed on a piece of paper and the outline drawn. Then measurements are taken of the instep, ankle, and calf, as I want riding boots. Old-fashioned they will probably continue until the end of time, yet somehow I sort of felt that if that old shop had a tongue to put in its cheek, there it would be parked, because tradition, as an aid to the cash register, is no novelty.

In the evening I dined at the Embassy Club with Sonny, and was made an honorary member of the club.

It is amazing how much Europe is aping America, particularly with its dance music. In cafés you hear all the popular airs that are being played on Broadway. The American influence has been felt to such an extent that King Jazz is a universal potentate. Sonny and I go to the theatre and see a part of the "League of Notions," but we leave early and I run to say hello to Constance Collier, who is playing in London.

The next day is exciting. Through the invitation of a third party I am to meet H. G. Wells at Stoll's office to view the first showing of Wells's picture, "Kipps."

In the morning the telephone rings and I hear some one in the parlour say that the Prince of Wales is calling. I get in a blue funk, as does everyone else in the apartment, and I hear them rush toward the 'phone. But Ed. Knoblock claiming to be versed in the proper method of handling such a situation, convinces everyone that he is the one to do the talking and I relapse back into bed, but wider awake than I ever was in my life.

Knoblock on the 'phone:

"Are you there? ... Yes ... Oh, yes ... to-night ... Thank you."

Knoblock turning from the 'phone announces, very formally, "The Prince of Wales wishes Charlie to dine with him to-night," and he starts toward my bedroom door. (Through all of this I have been in the bedroom, and the others are in the parlour confident, with the confidence of custom, that I am still asleep.)

As Knoblock starts for my bedroom door my very American secretary, in the very routine voice he has trained for such occurrences, says:

"Don't wake him. Tell him to call later. Not before two o'clock."

Knoblock: "Good God man! This is the Prince of Wales," and he launches into a monologue regarding the traditions of England and the customs of Court and what a momentous occasion this is, contemptuously observing that I am in bed and my secretary wants him to tell the Prince to call later! He cannot get the American viewpoint.

Knoblock's sincere indignation wins, and the secretary backs away from the bedroom as I plunge under the covers and feign sleep. Knoblock comes in very dignified and, trying to keep his voice in the most casual tone, announces, "Keep to-night open to dine with the Prince of Wales."

I try to enter into it properly, but I feel rather stiff so early in the morning. I try to remonstrate with him for having made the engagement. I have another engagement with H. G. Wells, but I am thrilled at the thought of dining with the Prince in Buckingham Palace. I can't do it. What must I do?

Knoblock takes me in hand. He repeats the message. I think some one is spoofing and tell him so. I am very suspicious, and the thrill leaves me as I remember that the Prince is in Scotland, shooting. How could he get back?

But Knoblock is practical. This must go through. And I think he is a bit sore at me for my lack of appreciation. He would go to the palace himself and find out everything. He goes to the palace to verify.

I can't tell his part of it—he was very vague—but I gathered that when he reached there he found all the furniture under covers, and I can hear that butler now saying:

"His Royal Highness the Prince will not be back for several days, sir."

Poor Ed.! It was quite a blow for him, and, on the level, I was a bit disappointed myself.

But I lost no time mooning over my lost chance to dine with royalty, for that afternoon I was going to meet Wells. Going to Stoll's; I was eagerly looking forward to a quiet little party where I could get off somewhere with Wells and have a long talk.

I meet H. G. Wells.

As I drew near the office, however, I noticed crowds, the same sort of crowds that I had been dodging since my exit from Los Angeles. It was a dense mass of humanity packed around the entire front of the building, waiting for something that had been promised them. And then I knew that it was an arranged affair and that, so far as a chat was concerned, Wells and I were just among those present, even though we were the guests of honour.

I remember keenly the crush in the elevator, a tiny little affair built for about six people and carrying nearer sixty. I get the viewpoint of a sardine quite easily. Upstairs it is not so bad, and I am swept into a room where there are only a few people and the door is then closed. I look all around, trying to spot Wells. There he is.

I notice his beautiful, dark-blue eyes first. Keen and kindly they are, twinkling just now as though he were inwardly smiling, perhaps at my very apparent embarrassment.

Before we can get together, however, there comes forward the camera brigade with its flashlight ammunition. Would we pose together? Wells looks hopeless. I must show that before cameras I am very much of a person, and I take the initiative with the lens peepers.

We are photoed sitting, standing, hats on and off, and in every other stereotyped position known to camera men.

We sign a number of photos, I in my large, sweeping, sprawling hand—I remember handling the pen in a dashing, swashbuckling manner—then Wells, in his small, hardly discernible style. I am very conscious of this difference, and I feel as though I had started to sing aloud before a group of grand-opera stars.

Then there is a quick-sketch artist for whom we pose. He does his work rapidly, however, and while he is drawing Wells leans over and whispers in my ear.

"We are the goats," he tells me. "I was invited here to meet you and you were probably invited here to meet me."

He had called the turn perfectly, and when we had both accepted the invitation our double acceptance had been used to make the showing an important event. I don't think that Wells liked it.

Wells and I go into the dark projection room and I sit with Wells. I feel on my mettle almost immediately, sitting at his side, and I feel rather glad that we are spending our first moments in an atmosphere where I am at home. In his presence I feel critical and analytical and I decide to tell the truth about the picture at all costs. I feel that Wells would do the same thing about one of mine.

As the picture is reeling off I whisper to him my likes and dislikes, principally the faulty photography, though occasionally I detect bad direction. Wells remains perfectly silent and I begin to feel that I am not breaking the ice. It is impossible to get acquainted under these conditions. Thank God, I can keep silent, because there is the picture to watch and that saves the day.

Then Wells whispers, "Don't you think the boy is good?"

The boy in question is right here on the other side of me, watching his first picture. I look at him. Just starting out on a new career, vibrant with ambition, eager to make good, and his first attempt being shown before such an audience. As I watch he is almost in tears, nervous and anxious.

The picture ends. There is a mob clustering about. Directors and officials look at me. They want my opinion of the picture. I shall be truthful. Shall I criticise? Wells nudges me and whispers, "Say something nice about the boy." And I look at the boy and see what Wells has already seen and then I say the nice things about him. Wells's kindness and consideration mean so much more than a mere picture.

Wells is leaving and we are to meet for dinner, and I am left alone to work my way through the crush to the taxi and back to the hotel, where I snatch a bit of a nap. I want to be in form for Wells.

There comes a little message from him:

Don't forget the dinner. You can wrap up in a cloak if you deem it advisable, and slip in about 7.30 and we can dine in peace.

H.   G.   Wells.
Whitehall Court, Entrance

We talk of Russia and I find no embarrassment in airing my views, but I soon find myself merely the questioner. Wells talks; and, though he sees with the vision of a dreamer, he brings to his views the practical. As he talks he appears very much like an American. He seems very young and full of "pep."

There is the general feeling that conditions will right themselves in some way. Organisation is needed, he says, and is just as important as disarmament. Education is the only salvation, not only of Russia, but of the rest of the world. Socialism of the right sort will come through proper education. We discuss my prospects of getting into Russia. I want to see it. Wells tells me that I am at the wrong time of the year, that the cold weather coming on would make the trip most inadvisable.

I talk about going to Spain, and he seems surprised to hear that I want to see a bull fight. He asks, "Why?"

I don't know, except that there is something so nakedly elemental about it. There is a picturesque technique about it that must appeal to any artist. Perhaps Frank Harris's "Matador" gave me the impulse, together with my perpetual quest for a new experience. He says it is too cruel to the horses.

I relax as the evening goes on and I find that I am liking him even more than I expected. About midnight we go out on a balcony just off his library, and in the light of a full moon we get a gorgeous view of London. Lying before us in the soft, mellow rays of the moon, London looks as though human, and I feel that we are rather in the Peeping Tom *rôle*.

I exclaim, "The indecent moon."

He picks me up. "That's good. Where did you get that?"

I have to admit that it is not original—that it belongs to Knoblock.

Wells comments on my dapperness as he helps me on with my coat. "I see you have a cane with you." I was also wearing a silk hat. I wonder what Los Angeles and Hollywood would say if I paraded there in this costume?

Wells tries on my hat, then takes my cane and twirls it. The effect is ridiculous, especially as just at the moment I notice the two volumes of the "Outline of History" on his table.

Strutting stagily, he chants, "You're quite the fellow doncher know."

We both laugh. Another virtue for Wells. He's human.

I try to explain my dress. Tell him that it is my other self, a reaction from the everyday Chaplin. I have always desired to look natty and I have spurts of primness. Everything about me and my work is so sensational that I must get reaction. My dress is a part of it. I feel that it is a poor explanation of the paradox, but Wells thinks otherwise.

He says I notice things. That I am an observer and an analyst. I am pleased. I tell him that the only way I notice things is on the run. Whatever keenness of perception I have is momentary, fleeting. I observe all in ten minutes or not at all.

What a pleasant evening it is! But as I walk along toward the hotel I feel that I have not met Wells yet.

And I am going to have another opportunity. I am going to have a week-end with him at his home in Easton, a week-end with Wells at home, with just his family. That alone is worth the entire trip from Los Angeles to Europe.

XI.

OFF TO FRANCE

The hotel next day is teeming with activity.

My secretaries are immersed in mail and, despite the assistance of six girls whom they have added temporarily to our forces, the mail bags are piling up and keeping ahead of us.

In a fit of generosity or ennui or something I pitch in and help. It seems to be the most interesting thing I have attempted on the trip. Why didn't I think of it sooner? Here is drama. Here is life in abundance. Each letter I read brings forth new settings, new characters, new problems. I find myself picking out many letters asking for charity. I lay these aside.

I have made up my mind to go to France immediately.

I call Carl Robinson. I tell him that we are going to France, to Paris, at once. Carl is not surprised. He has been with me for a long time. We decide that we tell nobody and perhaps we can escape ceremonies. We will keep the apartment at the Ritz and keep the stenographers working, so that callers will think that we are hiding about London somewhere.

We are going to leave on Sunday and our plans are perfected in rapid-fire order. We plunge about in a terrible rush as we try to arrange everything at the last minute without giving the appearance of arranging anything.

And in spite of everything, there is a mob at the station to see us off and autograph books are thrown at me from all sides. I sign for as many as I can and upon the others I bestow my "prop" grin. Wonder if I look like Doug when I do this?

We meet the skipper. What does one ask skippers? Oh yes, how does it look to-day for crossing? As I ask, I cast my weather eye out into the Channel and it looks decidedly rough for me.

But the skipper's "just a bit choppy" disarms me.

I am eager to get on the boat, and the first person I meet is Baron Long, owner of a hotel in San Diego. Good heavens! Can't I ever get away from Hollywood? I am glad to see him, but not now. He is very clever, however. He senses the situation, smiles quick "hellos," and then makes himself scarce. In fact, I think he wanted to get away himself. Maybe he was as anxious for a holiday as I.

I am approached on the boat by two very charming girls. They want my autograph. Ah, this is nice! I never enjoyed writing my name more.

How I wish that I had learned French. I feel hopelessly sunk, because after about three sentences in French I am a total loss so far as conversation is concerned. One girl promises to give me a French lesson. This promises to be a pleasant trip.

I am told that in France they call me Charlot. We are by this time strolling about the boat and bowing every other minute. It is getting rough and I find myself saying I rather like it that way. Liar.

She is speaking. I smile. She smiles. She is talking in French. I am getting about every eighth word. I cannot seem to concentrate, French is so difficult. Maybe it's the boat.

I am dying rapidly. I feel like a dead weight on her arm. I can almost feel myself get pale as I try to say something, anything. I am weak and perspiring. I blurt out, "I beg pardon," and then I rush off to my cabin and lie down. Oh, why did I leave England? Something smells horrible. I look up. My head is near a new pigskin bag. Yes, that's it, that awful leathery smell. But I have company. Robinson is in the cabin with me and we are matching ailments.

Thus we spent the trip from Dover to Calais and I was as glad to get to the French coast as the Kaiser would have been had he kept that dinner engagement in Paris.

Nearing France, I am almost forgetting my sickness. There is something in the atmosphere. Something vibrant. The tempo of life is faster. The springs in its mechanism are wound taut. I feel as if I would like to take it apart and look at those springs.

I am met by the chief of police, which surprised me, because I was confident that I had been canny enough to make a getaway this time. But no. The boat enters the quay and I see the dock crowded with people. Some treachery. Hats are waving, kisses are being thrown, and there are cheers. Cheers that I can only get through the expression, because they are in French and I am notoriously deficient in that language.

"*Vive le Charlot!*" "Bravo, Charlot!"

I am "Charloted" all over the place. Strange, this foreign tongue. Wonder why a universal language isn't practicable? They are crowding about me, asking for autographs. Or at least I think they are, because they are pushing books in my face, though for the life of me I can't make out a word of their chatter. But I smile. God bless that old "prop" grin, because they seem to like it.

Twice I was kissed. I was afraid to look around to see who did it, because I knew I was in France. And you've got to give me the benefit of the doubt. I am hoping that both kisses came from pretty girls, though I do think that at least one of those girls should shave.

They examine my signature closely. They seem puzzled. I look. It is spelled right. Oh, I see! They expected "Charlot." And I write some more with "Charlot."

I am being bundled along to a funny little French train. It seems like a toy. But I am enjoying the difference. Everything is all changed. The new money, the new language, the new faces, the new architecture—it's a grown-up three-ring circus to me. The crowd gives a concerted cheer as the train pulls out and a few intrepid ones run alongside until distanced by steam and steel.

We go into the dining-room and here is a fresh surprise. The dinner is *table d'hôte* and three waiters are serving it. Everyone is served at once, and as one man is taking up the soup plates another is serving the next course. Here is French economy—economy that seems very sensible as they have perfected it. It seems so different from America, where waiters always seem to be falling over one another in dining-rooms. And wines with the meal! And the check; it did not resemble in size the national debt, as dinner checks usually do in America.

It has started to rain as we arrive in Paris, which adds to my state of excitement, and a reportorial avalanche falls upon me. I am about overcome. How did reporters know I was coming? The crowd outside the station is almost as large as the one in London.

I am still feeling the effects of my sea-sickness. I am not equal to speaking nor answering questions. We go to the Customs house and one journalist, finding us, suggests and points another way out. I am sick. I must disappoint the crowd, and I leap into a taxi and am driven to Claridge's Hotel.

"Out of the frying pan." Here are more reporters. And they speak nothing but French. The hubbub is awful. We talk to one another. We shout at one another. We talk slowly. We spell. We do everything to make Frenchmen understand English, and Englishmen understand French, but it is no use. One of them manages to ask me what I think of Paris.

I answer that I never saw so many Frenchmen in my life. I am looking forward eagerly to meeting Cami, the famous French cartoonist. We have been corresponding for several years, he sending me many drawings and I sending him still photos from pictures. We had built up quite a friendship and I have been looking forward to a meeting. I see him.

He is coming to me and we are both smiling broadly as we open our arms to each other.

"Cami!"

"Charlot!"

Our greeting is most effusive. And then something goes wrong. He is talking in French, a blue streak, with the rapidity of a machine-gun. I can feel my smile fading into blankness. Then I get an inspiration. I start talking in English just as rapidly. Then we both talk at once. It's the old story of the irresistible force and the immovable body. We get nowhere.

Then I try talking slowly, extremely slow.

"Do—you—understand?"

It means nothing. We both realise at the same time what a hopeless thing our interview is. We are sad a bit, then we smile at the absurdity of it.

He is still Cami and I am still Charlot, so we grin and have a good time, anyhow.

He stays to dinner, which is a hectic meal, for through it all I am tasting this Paris, this Paris that is waiting for me. We go out and to the Folies Bergère. Paris does not seem as light as I expected it to be.

And the Folies Bergère seems shabbier. I remember having played here once myself with a pantomime act. How grand it looked then. Rather antiquated now. Somehow it saddened me, this bit of memory that was chased up before me.

Next day there is a luncheon with Dudley Field Malone and Waldo Frank. It is a brisk and vivacious meal except when it is broken up by a visit from the American newspaper correspondents.

"Mr. Chaplin, why did you come to Europe?"

"Are you going to Russia?"

"Did you call on Shaw?"

They must have cabled over a set of questions. I went all over the catechism for them and managed to keep the "prop" grin at work. I wouldn't let them spoil Paris for me.

We escape after a bit, and back at the hotel I notice an air of formality creeping into the atmosphere as I hear voices in the parlour of my suite. Then my secretary comes in and announces that a very important personage is calling and would speak with me.

He enters, an attractive-looking gentleman, and he speaks English.

"Mr. Chaplin, that I am to you talk of greetings from the heart of the people with France, that you make laugh. Cannot you forego to make showing of yourself with charity sometime for devastated France? On its behalf, I say to you——"

I tell him that I will take it up later.

He smiles, "Ah, you are boozy."

"Oh, no. I haven't had a drink for several days," I hasten to inform him. "I am busy and want to get to bed early to-night."

But Malone butts in with, "Oh yes, he's very boozy."

And I get a bit indignant until Malone tells me that the Frenchman means "busy."

Then I am told that there is one young journalist still waiting who has been here all day, refusing to go until I have seen him.

I tell them to bring him in. He comes in smiling in triumph.

And he can't speak English.

After his hours of waiting we cannot talk.

I feel rather sorry for him and we do our best. Finally, with the aid of about everyone in the hotel he manages to ask:—

"Do you like France?"

"Yes," I answer.

He is satisfied.

In Paris with Sir Philip Sassoon and Georges Carpentier.

Waldo Frank and I sit on a bench in the Champs Elysées and watch the wagons going to market in the early morning. Paris seems most beautiful to me just at this time.

What a city! What is the force that has made it what it is? Could anyone conceive such a creation, such a land of continuous gaiety? It is a masterpiece among cities, the last word in pleasure. Yet I feel that something has happened to it, something that they are trying to cover by heightened plunges into song and laughter.

We stroll along the boulevard and it is growing light. I am recognised and we are being followed. We are passing a church. There is an old woman asleep on the steps, but she does not seem worn and haggard. There is almost a smile on her face as she sleeps. She typifies Paris to me. Hides her poverty behind a smile.

Sir Philip Sassoon, who is the confidential secretary to Lloyd George, calls the next day with Georges Carpentier, the pugilistic idol of France, and we are photographed many times, the three of us together, and separately.

I am quite surprised that Sir Philip is such a young man. I had pictured the secretary of Lloyd George as rather a dignified and aged person. He makes an appointment for me to dine with Lord and Lady Rocksavage the next day. Lady Rocksavage is his sister.

I also lunch with them the next day, and then to a very fashionable modiste's for some shopping. This is my first offence of this sort. I meet Lady Astor, who is shopping there also.

It was quite a treat for me, watching the models in this huge, elaborate institution that was really a palace in appointments. In fact, it greatly resembled the palace at Versailles.

I felt very meek when tall, suave creatures strolled out and swept past me, some imperious, some contemptuous. It was a studied air, but they did it well. I wonder what effect it has on the girl's mind as she parades herself before the high-born ladies and gentlemen.

But I catch the imperfection in their schooling. It is very amusing to watch them strut about until their display is made, and then, their stunt done, slouch back into the dressing-rooms *sans* carriage and manner.

And then, too, I am discovered. This also causes a break in the spell of their queenly stroll. They are laughing and at the same time trying to maintain the dignity due to the gowns they are wearing. They become self-conscious and the effect is ludicrous.

I am demoralising the institution, so we get away. I would like to talk to some of the models, but it can't be done very well.

From there we go to a candy store, where I lay in a supply of chocolates and preserved fruits for my trip into Germany the next day. I am invited by Sir Philip to visit him at his country home in Lympne, Kent, on my return from Germany.

That evening I go with a party of Dudley Field Malone's to the Palais Royale in the Montmartre district. This is a novelty. Different. Seems several steps ahead of America. And it has atmosphere, something entirely its own, that you feel so much more than you do the tangible things about you.

There is a woman wearing a monocle. A simple touch, but how it changes! The fashions here proclaim themselves even without comparison and expert opinion.

The music is simple, exotic, neurotic. Its simplicity demands attention. It reaches inside you instead of affecting your feet.

They are dancing a tango. It is entertainment just to watch them. The pauses in the music, its dreamy cadences, its insinuation, its suggestiveness, its whining, almost monotonous swing. It is tropical yet, this Paris. And I realise that Paris is at a high pitch. Paris has not yet had relief from the cloddy numbness brought on with the War. I wonder will relief come easily or will there be a conflagration.

I meet Doughie, the correspondent. We recall our first meeting in the kitchen of Christine's in Greenwich Village.

It is soon noised about that I am here and our table takes on the atmosphere of a reception. What a medley!

Strangely garbed artists, long-haired poets, news-sheet and flower vendors, sightseers, students, children, and cocottes. Presently came a friend whom it was good to see again and we fix up a bit of a party and get into Dudley's petrol wagon, and as we bowl along we sing songs, ancient songs of the music-halls. "After the Ball," "The Man That Broke the Bank of Monte Carlo," and many another which I had not thought of in years.

Presently the wagon becomes balky and will not continue. So we all pile out and into a tavern near by, where we call for wine.

And Dudley played upon the tin-pan-sounding piano. There came one, a tall, strange, pale youth, who asked if we would like to go to the haunt of the Agile Rabbit. Thence uphill and into a cavernous place. When the patron came the youth ordered wine for us. Somehow I think he sensed the fact that I wanted to remain incognito.

The patron was such a perfect host. Ancient and white bearded, he served us with a finesse that was pure artistry. Then at his command one named Réné Chedecal, with a sad, haunted face, played upon the violin.

That little house sheltered music that night. He played as if from his soul, a message—yearning, passionate, sad, gay, and we were speechless before the emotional beauty and mystery of it.

I was overcome. I wanted to express my appreciation, but could do no more than grasp his hand. Genius breeds in strange places and humble.

And then the bearded one sang a song that he said the followers of Lafayette had sung before they left France for America. And all of us joined in the chorus, singing lustily.

Then a young chap did two songs from Verlaine, and a poet with considerable skill recited from his own poems. How effective for the creator of a thought to interpret it. And afterward the violin player gave us another selection of great beauty, one of his own compositions.

Then the old patron asked me to put my name in his ledger, which contained many names of both humble and famous. I drew a picture of my hat, cane, and boots, which is my favourite autograph. I wrote, "I would sooner be a gipsy than a movie man," and signed my name.

Home in the petrol wagon, which by this time had become manageable again. An evening of rareness. Beauty, excitement, sadness and contact with human, lovable personalities.

Waldo Frank called the next day, bringing with him Jacques Copeau, one of the foremost dramatists and actors in France, who manages and directs in his own theatre. We go to the circus together and I never saw so many sad-faced clowns. We dine together, and late that night I have supper with Copeau's company in a café in the Latin Quarter. It is a gay night, lasting until about three in the morning.

Frank and I set out to walk home together, but the section is too fascinating. Along about four o'clock we drift into another café, dimly lit but well lattended. We sit there for some time, studying the various occupants.

Over in one corner a young girl has just leaned over and kissed her sailor companion. No one seems to notice. All the girls here seem young, but their actions stamp their vocations. Music, stimulating, exotic, and for the dance, is being played. The girls are very much alive. They are putting their hats on the men's heads.

There are three peasant farmer boys, in all probability. They seem very much embarrassed as three tiny girls, bright-eyed and red-lipped, join them for a drink. I can see fire smouldering in their dull faces in spite of their awkwardness in welcoming the girls.

An interesting figure, Corsican, I should say, is very conspicuous. A gentleman by his bearing, debonair and graceful, he looks the very picture of an impecunious count. He is visiting all the tables in the café. At most of them he calls the girls by their first names.

He is taking up a collection for the musicians. Everyone is contributing liberally. With each tinkle of a coin in the hat the Corsican bows elaborately and extends thanks.

He finishes the collection.

"On with the dance," he shouts. "Don't let the music stop," as he rattles the money. Then he puts his hand in his pocket and draws forth a single centime piece. It is very small, but his manner is that of a philanthropist.

"I give something, no matter how small; you notice, ladies and gentlemen, that I give something," and he drops his coin in the hat and bows.

The party progresses rapidly. They have started singing and have had just enough drink to make them maudlin. We leave.

XII.

MY VISIT TO GERMANY

The train to Germany left so late in the evening that it was impossible for me to see devastated France even though we passed through a considerable portion of it. Our compartment on the train is very stuffy and smelly and the train service is atrocious, food and sanitary conditions being intolerable after American train service.

Again there is a crowd at the station to see me off, but I am rather enjoying it. A beautiful French girl presents me with a bouquet of flowers with a cute little speech, or at least I suppose it was, because she looked very cute delivering it, and the pouts that the language gave to her red lips were most provocative. She tells me in delicious broken English that I look tired and sad, and I find myself yielding without a struggle to her suggestion.

We arrive at Joumont near the Belgian frontier along about midnight, and, like a message from home, there is a gang of American soldier boys at the station to greet me. And they are not alone, for French, Belgian, and British troops are also waving and cheering. I wanted to talk to the Belgians, and we tried it, but it was no use. What a pity!

But one of them had a happy inspiration and saved the day.

"Glass of beer, Charlot?"

I nod, smiling. And to my surprise they bring me beer, which I lift to my lips for politeness, and then drink it to the last drop in pure pleasure. It is very good beer.

There is a group of charming little Belgian girls. They are smiling at me shyly and I so want to say something to them. But I can't. Ah, the bouquet! Each little girl gets a rose and they are delighted.

"*Merci, merci*, monsieur." And they keep "merciing" and bowing until the train pulls out of the station, which emboldens them to join the soldiers in a cheer.

Through an opening between the railroad structures I see a brilliant lighting display. It is universal, this sign. Here is a movie in this tiny village. What a wonderful medium, to reach such an obscure town.

On the train I am being told that my pictures have not played in Germany, hence I am practically unknown there. This rather pleases me because I feel that I can relax and be away from crowds.

Everyone on the train is nice and there is no trouble. Conductors struggle with English for my benefit, and the Customs officers make but little trouble. In fact, we cross the border at three in the morning and I am asleep.

Next morning I find a note from the Customs man saying; "Good luck, Charlie. You were sleeping so soundly that I did not have the heart to wake you for inspection."

Germany is beautiful. Germany belies the war. There are people crowding the fields, tilling the soil, working feverishly all the time as our train rushes through. Men, women, and children are all at work. They are facing their problem and rebuilding. A great people, perverted for and by a few.

The different style of architecture here is interesting. Factories are being built everywhere. Surely this isn't conquered territory. I do not see much live stock in the fields. This seems strange.

A dining-car has been put on the train and the waiter comes to our compartment to let us know that we may eat. Here is a novelty. A seven-course dinner, with wine, soup, meat, vegetables, salad, dessert, coffee, and bread for twenty-eight cents. This is made possible by the low rate of exchange.

We go to the Adlon Hotel in Berlin and find that hostelry jammed, owing to the auto races which are being run off at this time. A different atmosphere here. It seems hard for me to relax and get the normal reaction to meeting people. They don't know me here. I have never been heard of. It interests me and I believe I resent it just a bit.

I notice how abrupt the Germans are to foreigners, and I detect a tinge of bitterness, too. I am wondering about my pictures making their début here. I question the power of my personality without its background of reputation.

I am feeling more restful under this disinterested treatment, but somehow I wish that my pictures had been shown here. The people at the hotel are very courteous. They have been told that I am the "white-headed boy and quite the guy in my home town." Their reactions are amusing. I am not very impressive-looking and they are finding it hard to believe.

There is quite a crowd in the lobby and a number of Americans and English. They are not long in finding me, and a number of English, French, and American reporters start making a fuss over me. The Germans just stand and look on, bewildered.

Carl von Weigand comes forward with the offer of the use of his office while I am here. The Germans are impressed with all this, but they show no enthusiasm. I am accepted in an offhand way as some one of importance and they let it go at that.

The Scala Theatre, where I spent the evening, is most interesting, though I think a bit antiquated when compared with English and American theatrical progress along the same lines. It seats about five thousand, mostly on one floor, with a very small balcony. It is of the variety-music-hall type, showing mostly "dumb" acts. Acts that do not talk or sing, like comic jugglers, acrobats, and dancers.

I am amused by a German comedian singing a song of about twenty verses, but the audience is enthused and voices its approval at every verse. During the intermission we have frankfurters and beer, which are served in the theatre. I notice the crowds. They go to the theatre there as a family. It is just that type of an affair.

I notice the different types of beauty, though beauty is not very much in evidence here. Here and there are a few pretty girls, but not many. It is interesting to watch the people strolling during the intermission, drinking lager and eating all sorts of food.

Leaving the theatre, we visit the Scala Café, a sort of impressionistic casino. The Scala is one of the largest cafés in Berlin, where the modernist style in architecture has been carried out fully.

The walls are deep mottled sea green, shading into light verdigris and emerald, leaning outward at an angle, thereby producing an effect of collapse and forward motion. The junction of the walls and the ceiling is broken into irregular slabs of stone, like the strata of a cave. Behind these the lights are hidden, the whole system of illumination being based on reflection.

The immense dislocation of the planes and angles of the vault-like ceiling is focused on the central point, the huge silver star or crystal bursting like an exploding bomb through the roof. The whole effect is weird, almost ominous. The shape of the room in its ground plan is itself irregular—the impression is that of a frozen catastrophe. Yet this feeling seems to be in accord with the mood of revellers in Germany to-day.

From there to the Palais Heinroth, the most expensive place in Berlin and the high spot of night life. It is conspicuous in its brilliance, because Berlin as a city is so badly lighted. At night the streets are dark and gloomy, and it is then that one gets the effect of war and defeat.

At the Heinroth everybody was in evening dress. We weren't. My appearance did not cause any excitement. We check our hats and coats and ask for a table. The manager shrugs his shoulders. There is one in the back, a most obscure part of the room. This brings home forcibly the absence of my reputation. It nettled me. Well, I wanted rest. This was it.

We are about to accept humbly the isolated table, when I hear a shriek and I am slapped on the back and there's a yell:

"Charlie!"

It is Al Kaufman of the Lasky Corporation and manager of the Famous Players studio in Berlin.

"Come over to our table. Pola Negri wants to meet you."

Again I come into my own. The Germans look on, wondering. I have created attention at last. I discover that there is an American jazz band in the place. In the middle of a number they stop playing and shout:

"Hooray for Charlie Chaplin!"

The proprietor shrugs his shoulders and the band resumes playing. I learn that the musicians are former American doughboys. I feel rather pleased that I have impressed the Germans in the place.

In our party were Rita Kaufman, wife of Al, Pola Negri, Carl Robinson, and myself.

Pola Negri is really beautiful. She is Polish and really true to the type. Beautiful jet-black hair, white, even teeth and wonderful coloring. I think it such a pity that such coloring does not register on the screen.

She is the centre of attraction here. I am introduced. What a voice she has! Her mouth speaks so prettily the German language. Her voice has a soft, mellow quality, with charming inflections. Offered a drink, she clinks my glass and offers her only English words, "Jazz boy Charlie."

Language again stumps me. What a pity! But with the aid of a third party we get along famously. Kaufman whispers: "Charlie, you've made a hit. She just told me that you are charming."

"You tell her that she's the loveliest thing I've seen in Europe." These compliments keep up for some time, and then I ask Kaufman how to say, "I think you are divine" in German. He tells me something in German and I repeat it to her.

She's startled and looks up and slaps my hand.

"Naughty boy," she says.

The table roars. I sense that I have been double-crossed by Kaufman. What have I said? But Pola joins in the joke, and there is no casualty. I learn later that I have said, "I think you are terrible." I decided to go home and learn German.

As I am going out the proprietor approaches and very formally addresses me: "I beg pardon, sir. I understand that you are a great man in the United States. Accept my apologies for not knowing, and the gates here are always open to you." I accept them formally, though through it all I feel very comic opera. I didn't like the proprietor.

I want to go through the German slums. I mention such a trip to a German newspaper man. I am told that I am just like every Londoner and New-Yorker who comes to Berlin for the first time; that I want the Whitechapel district, the Bowery of Berlin, and that there is no such district. Once upon a time there were hovels in Berlin, but they have long since disappeared.

This to me is a real step toward civilisation.

My newspaper friend tells me that he will give me the next best thing to the slums, and we go to Krogel. What a picture could be made here! I am fascinated as I wander through houses mounted on shaky stilts and courts ancient but cleanly.

Then we drove to Acker Street and gazed into courts and basements. In a café we talked to men and women and drank beer. I almost launched a new war when, wishing to pay a charge of one hundred and eighty marks, I pulled from my pocket a roll of fifty one-thousand-mark notes.

My friend paid the check quickly with small change and hustled me out, telling me of the hard faces and criminal types who were watching. He's probably right, but I love those poor, humble people.

We drove to the arbor colonies in the northern part of the city, stopping at some of the arbors to talk to the people. I feel that I would like to eat dinner here among these people, but I haven't sufficient courage to persuade my companion, who wouldn't think of it. Passing through the northern part of Berlin, I found many beauties which, my friend let me know, were not considered beautiful at all.

He even suggested that he show me something in contrast with all I had seen. I told him no, that it would spoil my whole viewpoint.

It has been rather a restful experience, going through the whole town without being recognised, but even as I am thinking it a fashionable lady and her young daughter pass, and by their smiles I know that I am again discovered.

And then we meet Fritz Kreisler and his wife, who are just leaving for Munich. We have quite a chat and then make tentative engagements to be carried out in Los Angeles on his next trip there.

I notice that the Germans seem to be scrupulously honest, or maybe this was all the more noticeable to me because of genial and unsuspicious treatment by a taxi driver. We left the cab many times and were gone as long as half an hour at a time, and out of sight, yet he always waited and never suggested that he be paid beforehand.

In the business section we pass many cripples with embittered, sullen looks on their faces. They look as though they had paid for something which they hadn't received.

We are approached by a legless soldier beggar in a faded German uniform. Here was the War's mark. These sights you will find on every side in Berlin.

I am presented with a police card to the Berliner Club, which is evidently a technicality by which the law is circumvented. Berlin is full of such night-life clubs. They are somewhat like the gatherings that Prohibition has brought to America.

There are no signs, however, from the outside of any activity, and you are compelled to go up dark passages and suddenly come upon gaily lit rooms very similar to Parisian cafés.

Dancing and popping corks are the first impression as I enter. We are taken in hand by two girls and they order drinks for us. The girls are very nervous. In fact, the whole night-life of this town seems to be nervous, neurotic, over-done.

The girls dance, but very badly. They do not seem to enjoy it and treat it as part of the job. They are very much interested in my friend, who seems to have the money for the party. On these occasions my secretary always carries the family roll, and they are paying much attention to him.

I sit here rather moody and quiet, though one of the girls works hard to cheer me up. I hear her asking Robinson what is the matter with me. I smile and become courteous. But, her duty done, she turns again to Robinson.

I am piqued. Where is that personality of mine? I have been told many times that I have it. But here it is convincingly shown that personality has no chance against "pursenality."

But I am beginning to get so much attention from my friends that one of the girls is noticing me. She senses that I am some one important, but she can't quite make it out.

"Who is this guy, an English diplomat?" she whispers to Robinson. He whispers back that I am a man of considerable importance in the diplomatic service. I smile benevolently and they become more interested.

I am treating her rather paternally and am feeling philosophical. I ask about her life. What is she doing with it? What ambitions? She is a great reader, she tells me, and likes Schopenhauer and Nietzsche. But she shrugs her shoulders in an indifferent and tragic manner and says, "What does it matter about life?"

"You make it what it is," she says. "In your brain alone it exists and effort is only necessary for physical comfort." We are becoming closer friends as she tells me this.

But she must have some objective, there must be some dreams of the future still alive within her. I am very anxious to know what she really thinks.

I ask her about the defeat of Germany. She becomes discreet at once. Blames it on the Kaiser. She hates war and militarism. That's all I can get out of her, and it is getting late and we must leave. Her future intrigues me, but does not seem to worry her.

On the way home we step in at Kaufman's apartment and have quite a chat about pictures and things back in Los Angeles. Los Angeles seems very far away.

I am invited to a formal dinner party for the next evening at the home of Herr Werthauer, one of the most prominent lawyers in all Europe and a chief of the Kaiser during the war. The occasion for the dinner was to celebrate the announcement of Werthauer's engagement to his third wife.

His is a wonderful home in the finest section of Berlin. At the party there are a number of his personal friends, Pola Negri, Al Kaufman, Mrs. Kaufman, Robinson, and myself.

There is a Russian band playing native music all through the dinner and jazz music is also being dispensed by two orchestras made up of American doughboys who have been discharged, but have stayed on in Germany.

For no reason at all, I think of the story of Rasputin. This seems the sort of house for elaborate murders. Perhaps it is the Russian music that is having this effect on me. There is a huge marble staircase whose cold austereness suggests all sorts of things designed to send chills up the spine. The servants are so impressive and the meal such a ceremony that I feel that I am in a palace. The Russian folk-songs that are being dreamily whined from the strings of their peculiar instruments have a very weird effect and I find food and dining the least interesting things here.

There is a touch of mystery, of the exotic, something so foreign though intangible, that I find myself searching everything and everybody, trying to delve deeper into this atmosphere.

We are all introduced, but there are too many people for me to try to remember names. There are herrs, fräuleins, and fraus galore, and I find it hard to keep even their sex salutations correct. Some one is making a long, formal speech in German, and everybody is watching him attentively.

The host arises and offers a toast to his bride-to-be. Everyone rises and drinks to their happiness. The party is very formal and I can make nothing from the talk going on all about me. The host is talking and then all get up again with their glasses. Why, I don't know, but I get up with them.

At this there is general laughter, and I wonder what calamity has befallen me. I wonder if my clothes are all right.

Then I understand. The host is about to toast me. He does it in very bad English, though his gestures and tone make it most graceful. He is inclined to be somewhat pedantic and whenever he cannot think of the proper English word he uses its German equivalent.As the various courses come the toasts are many. I am always about two bites late in getting to my feet with my glass. After I have been toasted about four times, Mrs. Kaufman leans over and whispers, "You should toast back again to the host and say something nice about his bride-to-be."

I am almost gagged with the stage fright that grips me. It is the custom to toast back to the host and here I have been gulping down all kinds of toasts without a word. And he had been sitting there waiting for me.

I rise and hesitate. "Mr.—"

I feel a kick on the shins and I hear Mrs. Kaufman whisper hoarsely:

"Herr."

I think she means the bride-to-be. "Mrs.—" No, she isn't that yet. Heavens! this is terrible.

I plunge in fast and furious. "My very best respects to your future wife." As I speak I look at a young girl at the head of the table whom I thought was the lucky woman. I am all wrong. I sit, conscious of some horrible mistake.

He bows and thanks me. Mrs. Kaufman scowls and says: "That's not the woman. It's the one on the other side."

I have a suppressed convulsion and almost die, and as she points out the real bride-to-be I find myself laughing hysterically into my soup. Rita Kaufman is laughing with me. Thank heaven for a sense of humour.

I am so weak and nervous that I am almost tempted to leave at once. The bride-to-be is reaching for her glass to return my salute, though unless she thinks I am cross-eyed I don't see how she knows I said anything nice to her.

But she gets no chance to speak. There is launched a long-winded pedantic speech from the host, who says that on such rare occasions as this it is customary to uncork the best in the cellar. This point gets over in great shape and everybody is smiling.

I even feel myself growing radiant. I was under the impression that the best had already been served. Didn't know he was holding back anything. With the promise of better wine I am tempted to try another toast to the bride-to-be.

XIII.

I FLY FROM PARIS TO LONDON

The first night in Paris after our return from Germany we dined at Pioccardi's, then walked up to the arches of the old gates of Paris. Our intention was to visit the Louvre and see the statue of Venus de Milo, but it only got as far as intention.

We drifted into the Montmartre district and stopped in Le Rat Mort, one of its most famous restaurants. As it is very early in the evening, there are very few people about—one reason why I picked out this place, which later in the night becomes the centre of hectic revelry.

Passing our table is a striking-looking girl with bobbed blond hair, shadowing beautiful, delicate features of pale coloring and soft, strange eyes of a violet blue. Her passing is momentary, but she is the most striking-looking girl I have seen in Europe.

Although there are but few people here, I am soon recognised. The French are so demonstrative. They wave, "Hello, Charlot!"

I am indifferent. I smile mechanically. I am tired. I shall go to bed early. I order champagne.

The bobbed-hair one is sitting at a table near us. She interests me. But she doesn't turn so that I can see her face. She is sitting facing her friend, a dark, Spanish-looking girl.

I wish she'd turn. She has a beautiful profile, but I would like to see her full face again. She looked so lovely when she passed me before. I recall that ghost of a smile that hovered near her mouth, showing just a bit of beautiful, even, white teeth.

The orchestra is starting and dancers are swinging on to the floor. The two girls rise and join the dance. I will watch closely now and perhaps get another flash at her when she whirls by.

There is something refined and distinguished about the little girl. She is different. Doesn't belong here. I am watching her very closely, though she has never once looked my way. I like this touch of the unusual in Montmartre. Still she may be just clever.

She is passing me in the dance and I get a full view of her face. One of real beauty, with a sensitive mouth, smiling at her friend and giving a complete view of the beautiful teeth. Her face is most expressive. The music stops and they sit at their table.

I notice that there is nothing on their table. They are not drinking. This is strange, here. Nor are there sandwiches or coffee. I wonder who they are. That girl is somebody. I know it.

She gets up as the orchestra plays a few strains of a plaintive Russian thing. She is singing the song. Fascinating! An artist! Why is she here? I must know her.

The song itself is plaintive, elemental, with the insinuating nuances that are vital to Russian music. The orchestra, with the violins and 'cellos predominant, is playing hauntingly, weaving a foreign exotic spell.

She has poise, grace, and is compelling attention even in this place. There comes a bit of melancholy in the song and she sings it as one possessed, giving it drama, pathos. Suddenly there is a change. The music leaps to wild abandon. She is with it. She tosses her head like a wild Hungarian gipsy and gives fire to every note. But almost as it began, the abandon is over. With wistful sweetness, she is singing plaintively again.

She is touching every human emotion in her song. At times she is tossing away care, then gently wooing, an elusive strain that is almost fairylike, that crescendos into tragedy, going into a crashing climax that diminishes into an ending, searching yearning, and wistfully sad.

Her personality is written into every mood of the song. She is at once fine, courageous, pathetic, and wild. She finished to an applause that reflected the indifference of the place. In spots it was spontaneous and insistent. In others little attention was paid to her. She is wasted here.

But she cares not. In her face you can see that she gets her applause in the song itself. It was glorious, just to be singing with heart, soul and voice. She smiles faintly, then sits down modestly.

I knew it. She is Russian. She has everything to suggest it. Full of temperament, talent and real emotional ability, hidden away here in Le Rat Mort. What a sensation she would be in America with a little advertising! This is just a thought, but all sorts of schemes present themselves to me.

I can see her in "The Follies" with superb dressing and doing just the song she had done then. I did not understand a word of it, but I felt every syllable. Art is universal and needs no language. She has everything from gentleness to passion and a startling beauty. I am applauding too much, but she looks and smiles, so I am repaid.

They dance again, and while they are gone I call the waiter and have him explain to the manager that I would like to be presented to her. The manager introduces her and I invite her to my table. She sits there with us, while her companion, the dark girl, does a solo dance.

She talks charmingly and without restraint. She speaks three languages—Russian, French, and English. Her father was a Russian general during the Tsar's reign. I can see now where she gets her imperious carriage.

"Are you a Bolshevik?"

She flushes as I ask it, and her lips pout prettily as she struggles with English. She seems all afire.

"No, they are wicked. Bolshevik man, he's very bad." Her eyes flash as she speaks.

"Then you are bourgeoisie?"

"No, but not a Bolshevik." Her voice suggests a tremendous vitality, though her vocabulary is limited. "Bolshevik good idea for the mind, but not for practice."

"Has it had a fair opportunity?" I ask her.

"Plenty. My father, my mother, my brother all in Russia and very poor. Mother is Bolshevik, father bourgeoisie. Bolshevik man very impudent to me. I want to kill him. He insult me. What can I do? I escape. Bolshevik good idea, but no good for life."

"What of Lenin?"

"Very clever man. He tried hard for Bolshevik—but no good for everybody—just in the head."

I learn that she was educated in a convent and that she had lost all trace of her people. She earns her living singing here. She has been to the movies, but has never seen me. She "is go first chance because I am nice man."

I ask her if she would like to go into moving pictures. Her eyes light up.

"If I get opportunity I know I make success. But"—she curls her mouth prettily—"it's difficult to get opportunity."

She is just twenty years old and has been in the café for two weeks, coming there from Turkey, to which country she fled following her escape from Russia.

I explain that she must have photographic tests made and that I will try to get her a position in America. She puts everything into her eyes as she thanks me. She looks like a combination of Mary Pickford and Pola Negri plus her own distinctive beauty and personality. Her name is "Skaya." I write her full name and address in my book and promise to do all I can for her. And I mean to. We say "Good Night," and she says she feels that I will do what I say. How has she kept hidden?

Due at Sir Philip Sassoon's for a garden party the next day, I decide to go there in an aeroplane and I leave the Le Bourget aerodrome in Paris in a plane of La Compagnie des Messageries Aériennes, and at special request the pilot landed me at Lympne in Kent and I thereby avoided the crowd that would have been on hand in London.

It was quite thrilling and I felt that I made a very effective entrance to the party.

And what a delightful retreat! All the charm of an English country home, and Sir Philip is a perfect host. I get English food and treatment. I have a perfect rest, with no duties, and entertainment as I desire it. A day and a half that are most pleasant!

I meet Lady Rocksavage and Sir Philip Sassoon.

Next day there is to be a ceremonial in the schoolhouse, when a memorial is to be unveiled. It is in honour of the boys of the town who had fallen. There are mothers, fathers, and many old people, some of them old in years, others aged by the trials of the war.

The simple affair is most impressive and the streets are crowded on our way. I was to blame for an unhappy contrast. Outside people were shouting, "Hooray for Charlie!" while inside souls were hushed in grief.

Such a discordant note. I wished I had not been so prominent. I wanted everyone to bow in respect to these dead. The crowds did not belong outside.

And inside, on the little children's faces, I could see conflicting emotions. There is the reverence for the dead and yet there is eagerness as they steal glances at me. I wish I hadn't come. I feel that I am the disturbing element.

From the school Sir Philip and I went to the Star and Garter Hospital for wounded soldiers. Sheer tragedy was here.

Young men suffering from spinal wounds, some of them with legs withered, some suffering from shell shock. No hope for them, yet they smiled.

There was one whose hands were all twisted and he was painting signs with a brush held between his teeth. I looked at the signs. They were mottoes: "Never Say Die," "Are We Downhearted?" A superman.

Here is a lad who must take an anæsthetic whenever his nails are cut because of his twisted limbs. And he is smiling and to all appearances happy. The capacity that God gives for suffering is so tremendous, I marvel at their endurance.

I inquire about food and general conditions. They suggest that the food could be better. This is attended to.

We are received politely and with smiles from the crippled lads who are crippled in flesh only. Their spirit is boisterous. I feel a puny atom as they shout, "Good luck to you, Charlie."

I can't talk. There is nothing for me to say. I merely smile and nod and shake hands whenever this is possible. I sign autographs for as many as ask and I ask them to give me their autographs. I honestly want them.

One jovially says, "Sure, and Bill will give you one too." There is an uproar of laughter and Bill laughs just as loud as the rest. Bill has no arms.

But he bests them. He will sign at that. And he does. With his teeth. Such is their spirit. What is to become of them? That is up to you and me.

Back to Sir Philip's, very tired and depressed. We dine late and I go to my room and read Waldo Frank's "Dark Mothers." The next day there is tennis and music and in the evening I leave for London, where I am to meet H. G. Wells and go with him to his country home.

I am looking forward to this Saturday, Sunday, and Monday as an intellectual holiday. I meet H. G. at Whitehall and he is driving his own car. He is a very good chauffeur, too.

We talk politics and discuss the Irish settlement and I tell him of my trip to Germany. That leads to a discussion of the depreciation in the value of the mark. What will be the outcome? Wells thinks financial collapse. He thinks that marks issued as they are in Germany will be worthless.

I am feeling more intimate and closer to him. There is no strain in talking, though I am still a bit self-conscious and find myself watching myself closely.

We are out in the country, near Lady Warwick's estate, and H. G. tells me how the beautiful place is going to seed; that parts of it are being divided into lots and sold.

The estate, with its live stock, is a show place. It is breeding time for the deer and from the road we can hear the stags bellowing. H. G. tells me they are dangerous at this time of the year.

At the gate of the Wells' estate a young lad of ten greets us with a jovial twinkling of the eye and a brisk manner. There is no mistaking him. He is H. G.'s son. There is the same moulding of the structure and the same rounded face and eyes. H. G. must have looked that way at his age.

"Hello, dad," as he jumps on the running board.

"This is Charlie," H. G. introduces me.

He takes my grip. "How do?" and I notice what a fine boy he is.

Mrs. Wells is a charming little lady with keen, soft eyes that are always smiling and apparently searching and seeking something. A real gentlewoman, soft voiced, also with humorous lines playing around her mouth.

Everyone seems busy taking me into the house, and once there H. G. takes me all over it, to my room, the dining-room, the sitting-room and, an extra privilege, to his study. "My workshop," he calls it.

"Here's where the great events in the history of the world took place?"

He smiles and says "yes." The "Outline of History" was born here.

The room is not yet finished, and it is being decorated around the fireplace by paintings made by himself and wife. "I paint a bit," he explains. There is also some tapestry woven by his mother.

"Here is a place if you want to escape when the strain is too much for you. Come here and relax."

I felt that this was his greatest hospitality. But I never used the room. I had a feeling about that, too.

The study is simple and very spare of furniture. There is an old-fashioned desk and I get the general impression of books, but I can remember but one, the dictionary. Rare observation on my part to notice nothing but a dictionary, and this was so huge as it stood on his desk that I couldn't miss it.

There is a lovely view from the house of the countryside, with wide stretches of land and lovely trees, where deer are roaming around unafraid.

Mrs. Wells is getting lunch and we have it outdoors. Junior is there, the boy—I call him that already. Their conversation is rapid, flippant. Father and son have a profound analytical discussion about the sting of a wasp as one of the insects buzzed around the table.

It is a bit strange to me and I cannot get into the spirit of it, though it is very funny. I just watch and smile. Junior is very witty. He tops his father with jokes, but I sense the fact that H. G. is playing up to him. There is a twinkle in H. G.'s eye. He is proud of his boy. He should be.

After lunch we walk about the grounds and I doze most of the afternoon in the summer-house. They leave me alone and I have my nap out.

A number of friends arrive later in the evening and we are introduced all around. Most of these are literary, and the discussion is learned. St. John Ervine, the dramatist and author of "John Ferguson," came in later in the evening.

Ervine discusses the possibility of synchronising the voice with motion pictures. He is very much interested. I explain that I don't think the voice is necessary, that it spoils the art as much as painting statuary. I would as soon rouge marble cheeks. Pictures are pantomimic art. We might as well have the stage. There would be nothing left to the imagination.

Another son comes in. He is more like his mother. We all decide to play charades and I am selected as one of the actors. I play Orlando, the wrestler, getting a lot of fun through using a coal hod as a helmet. Then Noah's Ark, with Junior imitating the different animals going into the ark, using walking sticks as horns for a stag, and putting a hat on the end of the stick for a camel, and making elephants and many other animals through adroit, quick changes. I played old Noah and opened an umbrella and looked at the sky. Then I went into the ark and they guessed.

Then H. G. Wells did a clog dance, and did it very well. We talked far into the night, and I marvelled at Wells's vitality. We played many mental guessing games and Junior took all the honours.

I was awakened next morning by a chorus outside my door: "We want Charlie Chaplin." This was repeated many times. They had been waiting breakfast half an hour for me.

After breakfast we played a new game of H. G.'s own invention. Everyone was in it and we played it in the barn. It was a combination of handball and tennis, with rules made by H. G. Very exciting and good fun.

Then a walk to Lady Warwick's estate. As I walk I recall how dramatic it had sounded last night as I was in bed to hear the stags bellowing, evidently their cry of battle.

The castle, with beautiful gardens going to seed, seemed very sad, yet its ruins assumed a beauty for me. I liked it better that way. Ruins are majestic.

H. G. explains that everyone about is land poor. It takes on a fantastic beauty for me, this cultivation of centuries now going to seed, beautiful in its very tragedy.

Home for tea, and in the evening I teach them baseball. Here is my one chance to shine. It is funny to see H. G. try to throw a curve and being caught at first base after hitting a grounder to the pitcher. H. G. pitched, and his son caught. As a baseball player H. G. is a great writer. Dinner that night is perfect, made more enjoyable for our strenuous exercise. As I retire that night I think of what a wonderful holiday I am having.

Next day I must leave at 2.30 p.m., but in the morning H. G. and I take a walk and visit an old country church built in the eleventh century. A man is working on a tomb-stone in the churchyard, engraving an epitaph.

H. G. points out the influence of the different lords of the manor on the art changes of different periods. Here the families of Lady Warwick and other notable people are buried. The tombstones show the influence of the sculpture of all periods.

We go to the top of the church and view the surrounding country and then back home for lunch. My things are all packed and H. G. and his son see me off. H. G. reminds me not to forget another engagement to dine with him and Chaliapin, the famous Russian baritone.

As I speed into town I am wondering if Wells wants to know me or whether he wants me to know him. I am certain that now I have met Wells, really met him, more than I've met anyone in Europe. It's so worth while.

XIV.

FAREWELLS TO PARIS AND LONDON

I had promised to attend the *première* showing of "The Kid" in Paris, and I went back to the French capital as I came, via aeroplane. The trip was uneventful, and on landing and going to my hotel I find a message from Doug Fairbanks. He and Mary had arrived in Paris and were stopping at the Crillon. They asked me over for a chat but I was too tired. Doug promised to attend the *première* at the Trocadero Theatre.

During the afternoon there came souvenir programmes to be autographed. These were to be sold that night for francs each.

In the evening I went to the theatre *via* the back way, but there was no escape. It was the biggest demonstration I had yet seen. For several blocks around the crowds were jammed in the streets and the gendarmes had their hands full.

Paris had declared a holiday for this occasion, and as the proceeds of the entertainment were to be given to the fund for devastated France the élite of the country were there. I am introduced to Ambassador Herrick, then shown to my box and introduced to the Ministers of the French Cabinet.

I do not attempt to remember names, but the following list has been preserved for me by my secretary:

M. Menard, who attended on behalf of President Millerand; M. Jusserand, M. Herbette, M. Careron, M. Loucheur, Minister of the Liberated Regions; M. Hermite, Col. and Mrs. H. H. Harjes, Miss Hope Harjes, Mr. and Mrs. Ridgeley Carter, Mrs. Arthur James, Mrs. W. K. Vanderbilt, Mrs. Rutherford Stuyvesant, Walter Berry, M. de Errazu, Marquis de Vallambrosa, Mlle. Cecile Sorel, Robert Hostetter, M. Byron-Kuhn, Mr. and Mrs. Charles G. Loeb, Florence O'Neill, M. Henri Lettelier, M. Georges Carpentier, Paul C. Otey, Mr. and Mrs. George Kenneth End, Prince George of Greece, Princess Xenia, Prince Christopher, Lady Sarah Wilson, Mrs. Elsa Maxwell, Princess Sutzo, Vice-Admiral and Mrs. Albert P. Niblack, Comte and Comtesse Cardelli, Duchess de Talleyrand, Col. and Mrs. N. D. Jay, Col. Bunau Varila, Marquise de Talleyrand-Périgord, Marquis and Marquise de Chambrun, Miss Viola Cross, Miss Elsie De Wolf, Marquis and Marquise de Dampierre, and Mr. and Mrs. Theodore Rousseau.

My box is draped with American and British flags, and the applause is so insistent that I find I am embarrassed. But there is a delicious tingle to it and I am feeling now what Doug felt when his "Three Musketeers" was shown. The programmes which I autographed during the afternoon are sold immediately and the audience wants more. I autograph as many more as possible.

I am photographed many times and I sit in a daze through most of it, at one time going back stage, though I don't know why, except that I was photoed back there too.

The picture was shown, but I did not see much of it. There was too much to be seen in that audience.

At the end of the picture there came a messenger from the Minister:

"Would I come to his box and be decorated?" I almost fell out of my box.

I grew sick. What would I say? There was no chance to prepare. I had visions of the all-night preparation for my speech in Southampton. This would be infinitely worse. I couldn't even think clearly. Why do I pick out stunts like that? I might have known that something would happen.

But the floor would not open up for me to sink through and there was no one in this friendly audience who could help in my dilemma, and the messenger was waiting politely, though I imagined just a bit impatiently, so, summoning what courage I had, I went to the box with about the same feeling as a man approaching the guillotine.

I am presented to everybody. He makes a speech. It is translated for me, but very badly. While he was speaking I tried to think of something neat and appropriate, but all my thoughts seemed trite. I finally realised that he was finished and I merely said "*Merci*," which, after all, was about as good as I could have done.

And believe me, I meant "*Merci*" both in French and in English.

But the applause is continuing. I must say something, so I stand up in the box and make a speech about the motion-picture industry and tell them that it is a privilege for us to make a presentation for such a cause as that of devastated France.

Somehow they liked it, or made me believe they did. There was a tremendous demonstration and several bearded men kissed me before I could get out. But I was blocked in and the crowd wouldn't leave. At last the lights were turned out, but still they lingered. Then there came an old watchman who said he could take us through an unknown passage that led to the street.

We followed him and managed to escape, though there was still a tremendous crowd to break through in the street. Outside I meet Cami, who congratulates me, and together we go to the Hotel Crillon to see Doug and Mary.

Mary and Doug are very kind in congratulating me, and I tell them of my terrible conduct during the presentation of the decoration. I knew that I was wholly inadequate for the occasion. I keep mumbling of my *faux pas* and they try to make me forget my misery by telling me that General Pershing is in the next room.

I'll bet the general never went through a battle like the one I passed through that night.

Then they wanted to see the decoration, which reminded me that I had not yet looked at it myself. So I unrolled the parchment and Doug read aloud the magic words from the Minister of Instruction of the Public and Beaux Arts which made Charles Chaplin, dramatist, artist, an *Officier de L'instruction Publique*.

We sit there until three in the morning, discussing it, and then I go back to my hotel tired but rather happy. That night was worth all the trip to Europe.

At the hotel there was a note from Skaya. She had been to the theatre to see the picture. She sat in the gallery and saw "The Kid," taking time off from her work.

Her note:

"I saw picture. You are a grand man. My heart is joy. You must be happy. I laugh—I cry.

"Skaya."

This little message was not the least of my pleasures that night.

Elsie De Wolf was my hostess at luncheon next day at the Villa Trianon, Versailles, a most interesting and enjoyable occasion, where I met some of the foremost poets and artists.

Returning to Paris, I meet Henry Wales, and we take a trip through the Latin Quarter together. That night I dine with Cami, Georges Carpentier, and Henri Letellier. Carpentier asks for an autograph and I draw him a picture of my hat, shoes, cane, and moustache, my implements of trade. Carpentier, not to be outdone, draws for me a huge fist encased in a boxing glove.

I am due back in England next day to lunch with Sir Philip Sassoon and to meet Lloyd George. Lord and Lady Rocksavage, Lady Diana Manners, and many other prominent people are to be among the guests, and I am looking forward to the luncheon eagerly.

We are going back by aeroplane, though Carl Robinson lets me know that he prefers some other mode of travel. On this occasion I am nervous and I say frequently that I feel as though something is going to happen. This does not make a hit with Carl.

We figure that by leaving at eight o'clock in the morning we can make London by one o'clock, which will give me plenty of time to keep my engagement.

But we hadn't been up long before we were lost in the fog over the Channel and were forced to make a landing on the French coast, causing a delay of two hours. But we finally made it, though I was two hours late for my engagement, and the thought of keeping Lloyd George and those other people waiting was ghastly.

Our landing in England was made at the Croydon aerodrome, and there was a big automobile waiting outside, around which were several hundred people. The aerodrome officials, assuming that the car was for me, hustled me into it and it was driven off.

But it was not mine, and I found that I was not being driven to the Ritz, but the Majestic Theatre in Clapham.

The chauffeur wore a moustache, and, though he looked familiar, I did not recognise him. But very dramatically he removed the moustache.

"I am Castleton Knight. A long time ago you promised me to visit my theatre. I have concluded that the only way to get you there is to kidnap you. So kindly consider yourself kidnapped."

I couldn't help but laugh, even as I thought of Lloyd George, and I assured Mr. Knight that he was the first one who had ever kidnapped me. So we went to the theatre, and I stayed an hour and surprised both myself and the audience by making a speech.

Back to my hotel Sir Philip meets me and tells me that Lloyd George couldn't wait, that he had a most important engagement at four o'clock. I explained the aeroplane situation to Sir Philip and he was very kind. I feel that it was most unfortunate, for it was my only opportunity to meet Lloyd George in these times, and I love to meet interesting personages. I would like to meet Lenin, Trotsky, and the Kaiser.

This is to be my last night in England, and I have promised to dine and spend the evening with my Cousin Aubrey. One feels dutiful to one's cousin.

I also discover that this is the day I am to meet Chaliapin and H. G. Wells. I phone H. G. and explain that this is my last day, and of my promise to my cousin. H. G. is very nice. He understands. You can only do these things with such people.

My cousin calls for me at dusk in a taxi and we ride to his home in Bayswater. London is so beautiful at this hour, when the first lights are being turned on, and each light to me is symbolical. They all mean life, and I wish sometimes I could peer behind all these lighted windows.

Reaching Aubrey's home I notice a number of people on the other side of the street standing in the shadows. They must be reporters, I think, and am slightly annoyed that they should find me even here. But my cousin explains hesitatingly that they are just friends of his waiting for a look at me.

I feel mean and naughty about this, as I recall that I had requested him not to make a party of my visit.

I just wanted a family affair, with no visitors, and these simple souls on the other side of the street were respecting my wishes. I relent and tell Aubrey to ask them over, anyway. They are all quite nice, simple tradesmen, clerks, etc.

Aubrey has a saloon, or at least a hotel, as he calls it, in the vicinity of Bayswater, and later in the evening I suggest that we go there and take his friends with us. Aubrey is shocked.

"No, not around to my place." Then they all demur. They don't wish to intrude. I like this. Then I insist. They weaken. He weakens.

We enter a bar. The place is doing a flourishing business. There are a number of pictures of my brother Syd and myself all over the walls, in character and straight. The place is packed to-night. It must be a very popular resort.

"What will you have?" I feel breezy. "Give the whole saloon a drink."

Aubrey whispers, "Don't let them know you are here." He says this for me.

But I insist. "Introduce me to all of them." I must get him more custom.

He starts quietly whispering to some of his very personal friends: "This is my cousin. Don't say a word."

I speak up rather loudly. "Give them all a drink." I feel a bit vulgar to-night. I want to spend money like a drunken sailor. Even the customers are shocked. They hardly believe that it's Charlie Chaplin, who always avoids publicity, acting in this vulgar way.

I am sure that some of them don't believe despite many assurances. A stunt of my cousin's. But they drink, reverently and with reserve, and then they bid me good night, and we depart quietly, leaving Bayswater as respectable as ever.

To the house for dinner, after which some one brings forth an old family album. It is just like all other family albums.

"This is your great-granduncle and that is your great-grandmother. This is Aunt Lucy. This one was a French general."

Aubrey says: "You know we have quite a good family on your father's side." There are pictures of uncles who are very prosperous cattle ranchers in South Africa. Wonder why I don't hear from my prosperous relations.

This is the first time that I am aware of my family and I am now convinced that we are true aristocrats, blue blood of the first water.

Aubrey has children, a boy of twelve, whom I have never met before. A fine boy. I suggest educating him. We talk of it at length and with stress. "Let's keep up family tradition. He may be a member of Parliament or perhaps President. He's a bright boy."

We dig up all the family and discuss them. The uncles in Spain. Why, we Chaplins have populated the earth.

When I came I told Aubrey that I could stay only two hours, but it is a.m. and we are still talking. As we leave Aubrey walks with me toward the Ritz.

We hail a Ford truck on the way and a rather dandified young Johnny, a former officer, gives us a lift.

"Right you are. Jump on."

A new element, these dandies driving trucks, some of them graduates of Cambridge and Oxford, of good families, most of them, impecunious aristocrats. Perhaps it is the best thing that could happen to such families.

This chap is very quiet and gentle. He talks mostly of his truck and his marketing, which he thinks is quite a game. He has been in the grocery business since the war and has never made so much money. We get a good bit of his story as we jolt along in the truck.

He is providing vegetables and fruit for all his friends in Bayswater, and every morning at four o'clock he is on his way to the market. He loves the truck. It is so simple to drive.

"Half a mo." He stops talking and pulls up for petrol at a pretty little white-tiled petrol station. The station is all lit up, though it is but

a.m.

"Good morning. Give me about five gal."

"Right-o!"

The cheery greeting means more than the simple words that are said.

The lad recognises me and greets me frankly, though formally. It seems so strange to me to hear this truck driver go along conversing in the easiest possible manner. A truck driver who enjoyed truck driving.

He spoke of films for just a bit and then discreetly stopped, thinking, perhaps, that I might not like to talk about them. And, besides, he liked to talk about his truck.

He told us how wonderful it was to drive along in the early morning with only the company of dawn and the stars. He loved the silent streets, sleeping London. He was enterprising, full of hopes and ambitions. Told how he bartered. He knew how. His was a lovely business.

He was smoking a pipe and wore a trilby hat, with a sort of frock coat, and his neck was wrapped in a scarf. I figured him to be about thirty years of age.

I nudged my cousin. Would he accept anything? We hardly know whether or not to offer it, though he is going out of his way to drive me to the Ritz.

He has insisted that it is no trouble, that he can cut through to Covent Garden. No trouble. I tell the petrol man to fill it up and I insist on paying for the petrol.

The lad protests, but I insist.

"That's very nice of you, really. But it was a pleasure to have you," he says, as he gets back in his seat.

We cut through to Piccadilly and pull up at the Ritz in a Ford truck. Quite an arrival.

The lad bids us good-bye. "Delighted to have met you. Hope you have a bully time. Too bad you are leaving. Bon voyage. Come back in the spring. London is charming then. Well, I must be off. I'm late. Good morning."

We talk him over on the steps as he drives away. He is the type of an aristocrat that must live. He is made of the stuff that marks the true aristocrat. He is an inspiration. He talked just enough, never too much. The intonation of his voice and his sense of beauty as he appreciated the dawn stamped him as of the élite—the real élite, not the Blue Book variety.

Loving adventure, virtuous, doing something all the time, and loving the doing. What an example he is! He has two stores. This is his first truck. He loves it. He is the first of his kind that I have met. This is my last night in England. I am glad that it brought me this contact with real nobility.

XV.

BON VOYAGE

I am off in the morning for Southampton, miserable and depressed. Crowds—the same crowds that saw me come—are there. But they seem a bit more desirable. I am leaving them. There are so many things I wish I had done. It is pleasant to be getting this applause on my exit.

I do not doubt its sincerity now. It is just as fine and as boisterous as it was when I arrived. They were glad to see me come and are sorry I am going.

I feel despondent and sad. I want to hug all of them to me. There is something so wistful about London, about their kind, gentle appreciation. They smile tenderly as I look this way, that way, over there—on every side it is the same. They are all my friends and I am leaving them.

Will I sign this? A few excited ones are shoving autograph books at me, but most of them are under restraint, almost in repose. They feel the parting. They sense it, but are sending me away with a smile.

My car is full of friends going with me to Southampton. They mean little at the moment. The crowd has me. Old, old friends turn up, friends that I have been too busy to see. Faithful old friends who are content just to get a glimpse before I leave.

There's Freddy Whittaker, an old music-hall artist with whom I once played. Just acquaintances, most of them, but they all knew me, and had all shared, in spirit, my success. All of them are at the station and all of them understand. They know that my life has been full every minute I have been here. There had been so much to do.

They knew and understood, yet they had come determined just to see me, if only at the door of my carriage. I feel very sad about them.

The train is about to pull out and everything is excitement. Everyone seems emotional and there is a tenseness in the very atmosphere.

"Love to Alf and Amy," many of them whisper, those who know my manager and his wife. I tell them that I am coming back, perhaps next summer. There is applause. "Don't forget," they shout. I don't think I could forget.

The trip to Southampton is not enjoyable. There is a sadness on the train. A sort of embarrassed sentimentality among my friends. Tom Geraghty is along. Tom is an old American and he is all choked up at the thought of my going back while he has to stay on in England. We are going back to his land. We cannot talk much.

We go to the boat. Sonny is there to see me off. Sonny, Hetty's brother.

There is luncheon with my friends and there are crowds of reporters. I can't be annoyed. There is nothing for me to say. I can't even think. We talk, small talk, joke talk.

Sonny is very matter-of-fact. I look at him and wonder if he has ever known. He has always been so vague with me. Has always met me in a joking way.

He leans over and whispers, "I thought you might like this." It is a package. I almost know without asking that it is a picture of Hetty. I am amazed. He understood all the time. Was always alive to the situation. How England covers up her feelings!

Everybody is off the boat but the passengers. My friends stand on the dock and wave to me. I see everything in their glowing faces—loyalty, love, sadness, a few tears. There is a lump in my throat. I smile just as hard as I can to keep them from seeing. I even smile at the reporters. They're darn nice fellows. I wish I knew them better. After all, it's their job to ask questions and they have been merely doing their job with me. Just doing their jobs, as they see it. That spirit would make the world if it were universal.

England never looked more lovely. Why didn't I go here? Why didn't I do this and that? There is so much that I missed. I must come back again. Will they be glad to see me? As glad as I am to see them? I hope so. My cheek is damp. I turn away and blot out the sadness. I am not going to look back again.

A sweet little girl about eight years of age, full of laughing childhood, is coming toward me with a bubbling voice. Her very look commands me not to try to escape. I don't think I want to escape from her.

"Oh, Mr. Chaplin," gurgled the little girl, "I've been looking for you all over the boat. Please adopt me like you did Jackie Coogan. We could smash windows together and have lots of fun. I love your plays."

She takes my hand and looks up into my face. "They are so clever and beautiful. Won't you teach me like you taught him? He's so much like you. Oh, if I could only be like him."

And with a rapt look on her little face she prattles on, leaving me very few opportunities to get in a word, though I prefer to listen to her rather than talk.

I wave good-bye to my friends and then walk along with her, going up and looking back at the crowd over the rail.

Reporters are here. They scent something interesting in my affair with the little girl. I answer all questions. Then a photographer. We are photographed together. And the movie men are getting action pictures. We are looking back at my friends on shore.

The little girl asks: "Are they all actors and in the movies? Why are you so sad? Don't you like leaving England? There will be so many friends in America to meet you. Why, you should be so happy because you have friends all over the world!"

I tell her that it is just the parting—that the thought of leaving is always sad. Life is always "Good-bye." And here I feel it is good-bye to new friends, that my old ones are in America.

We walk around the deck and she discusses the merits of my pictures.

"Do you like drama?" I ask.

"No. I like to laugh, but I love to make people cry myself. It must be nice to act 'cryie' parts, but I don't like to watch them."

"And you want me to adopt you?"

"Only in the pictures, like Jackie. I would love to break windows."

She has dark hair and a beautiful profile of the Spanish type, with a delicately formed nose and a Cupid's bow sort of mouth. Her eyes are sensitive, dark and shining, dancing with life and laughter. As we talk I notice as she gets serious she grows tender and full of childish love.

"You like smashing windows! You must be Spanish," I tell her.

"Oh no, not Spanish; I'm Jewish," she answers.

"That accounts for your genius."

"Oh, do you think Jewish people are clever?" she asks, eagerly.

"Of course. All great geniuses had Jewish blood in them. No, I am not Jewish," as she is about to put that question, "but I am sure there must be some somewhere in me. I hope so."

"Oh, I am so glad you think them clever. You must meet my mother. She's brilliant and an elocutionist. She recites beautifully, and is so clever at anything. And I am sure you would like my father. He loves me so much and I think he admires me some, too."

She chatters on as we walk around. Then suddenly. "You look tired. Please tell me and I will run away."

As the boat is pulling out her mother comes toward us and the child introduces us with perfect formality and without any embarrassment. She is a fine, cultured person.

"Come along, dear, we must go down to the second class. We cannot stay here."

I make an appointment to lunch with the little girl on the day after the morrow, and am already looking forward to it.

I spend the greater part of the second day in reading books by Frank Harris, Waldo Frank, Claude McKay, and Major Douglas's "Economic Democracy."

The next day I met Miss Taylor, a famous moving-picture actress of England, and Mr. Hepworth, who is a director of prominence in Great Britain. Miss Taylor, though sensitive, shy, and retiring, has a great bit of charm.

They are making their first trip to America, and we soon become good friends. We discuss the characteristics of the American people, contrasting their youthful, frank abruptness with the quiet, shy, and reserved Britisher.

I find myself running wild as I tell them of this land. I explain train hold-ups, advertising signs, Broadway lights, blatant theatres, ticket speculators, subways, the automat and its big sister, the cafeteria. It has a great effect on my friends and at times I almost detect unbelief. I find myself wanting to show the whole thing to them and to watch their reactions.

At luncheon next day the little girl is the soul of the party. We discuss everything from Art to ambitions. At one moment she is full of musical laughter, and the next she is excitedly discussing some happening aboard ship. Her stories are always interesting. How do children see so much more than grown-ups?

She has a great time. I must visit her father, he is so much like me. He has the same temperament, and is such a great daddy. He is so good to her. And she rattles on without stopping.

Then again she thinks I may be tired. "Sit back now." And she puts a pillow behind my head and bids me rest.

These moments with her make days aboard pass quickly and pleasantly.

Carl Robinson and I are strolling around the top deck the next day in an effort to get away from everyone, and I notice someone looking up at a wire running between the funnels of the ship. Perched on the wire is a little bird, and I am wondering how it got there and if it had been there since we left England.

The other watcher notices us. He turns and smiles. "The little bird must think this is the promised land."

I knew at once that he was somebody. Those thoughts belong only to poets. Later in the evening he joins us at my invitation and I learn he is Easthope Martin, the composer and pianist. He had been through the War and it had left its stamp on this fine, sensitive soul. He had been gassed. I could not imagine such a man in the trenches.

He is very frail of body, and as he talks I always imagine his big soul at the bursting point with a pent-up yearning.

There is the inevitable concert on the last night of the voyage. We are off the banks of Newfoundland, and in the midst of a fog. Fog horns must be kept blowing at intervals, hence the effect on the concert, particularly the vocal part, is obvious.

We land at seven in the morning of a very windy day, and it is eleven before we can get away. Reporters and camera men fill the air during all that time, and I am rather glad, because it shows Miss Taylor and Mr. Hepworth a glimpse of what America is like. We arrange to meet that night at Sam Goldwyn's for dinner.

Good-byes here are rather joyous, because we are all getting off in the same land and there will be an opportunity to see one another again.

My little friend comes to me excitedly and gives me a present—a silver stamp box. "I hope that when you write your first letter you take a stamp from here and mail it to me. Good-bye."

She shakes hands. We are real lovers and must be careful. She tells me not to overwork. "Don't forget to come and see us; you must meet daddy. Good-bye, Charlie."

She curtsies and is gone. I go to my cabin to wait until we can land. There is a tiny knock. She comes in.

"Charlie, I couldn't kiss you out there in front of all those people. Good-bye, dear. Take care of yourself." This is real love. She kisses my cheek and then runs out on deck.

Easthope Martin is with us that night at Goldwyn's party. He plays one of his own compositions and holds us spellbound. He is very grateful for our sincere applause and quite retiring and unassuming, though he is the hit of the evening.

Following the dinner I carried the English movie folk on a sight-seeing trip, enjoying their amazement at the wonders of a New York night.

"What do you think of it?" I asked them.

"Thrilling," says Hepworth. "I like it. There is something electrical in the air. It is a driving force. You must do things."

We go to a café, where the élite of New York are gathered, and dance until midnight. I bid them good-bye, hoping to meet them later when they come to Los Angeles.

I dine at Max Eastman's the next night and meet McKay, the negro poet. He is quite handsome, a full-blooded Jamaican negro not more than twenty-five years of age. I can readily see why he has been termed an African prince. He has just that manner.

I have read a number of his poems. He is a true aristocrat with the sensitiveness of a poet and the humour of a philosopher, and quite shy. In fact, he is rather supersensitive, but with a dignity and manner that seem to hold him aloof.

There are many other friends there, and we discuss Max's new book on humour. There is a controversy whether to call it "Sense of Humour" or "Psychology of Humour." We talk about my trip. Claude McKay asks if I met Shaw. "Too bad," he says. "You would like him and he would have enjoyed you."

I am interested in Claude. "How do you write your poetry? Can you make yourself write? Do you prepare?" I try to discuss his race. "What is their future? Do they——"

He shrugs his shoulders. I realise he is a poet, an aristocrat.

I dine the next evening with Waldo Frank and Marguerite Naumberg and we discuss her new system. She has a school that develops children along the lines of personality. It is a study in individuality. She is struggling alone, but is getting wonderful results. We talk far into the morning on everything, including the fourth dimension.

Next day Frank Harris calls and we decide to take a trip to Sing Sing together. Frank is very sad and wistful. He is anxious to get away from New York and devote time to his autobiography before it is too late. He has so much to say that he wants to write it while it is keen.

I try to tell him that consciousness of age is a sign of keenness. That age doesn't bother the mind.

We discuss George Meredith and a wonderful book he had written. And then in his age Meredith had rewritten it. He said it was so much better rewritten, but he had taken from it all the red blood. It was old, withered like himself. You can't see things as they were. Meredith had become old. Harris says he doesn't want the same experience.

All this on the way to Sing Sing. Frank is a wonderful conversationalist. Like his friend Oscar Wilde. That same charm and brilliancy of wit, ever ready for argument. What a fund of knowledge he has. What a biography his should be. If it is just half as good as Wilde's, it will be sufficient.

Sing Sing. The big, grey stone buildings seem to me like an outcry against civilisation. This huge grey monster with its thousand staring eyes. We are in the visiting room. Young men in grey shirts. Thank God, the hideous stripes are gone. This is progress, humanity. It is not so stark.

There is a mite of a baby holding her daddy's hand and playing with his hair as he talks with her mamma, his wife. Another prisoner holding two withered hands of an old lady. Mother was written all over her, though neither said a word. I felt brutal at witnessing their emotion.

All of them old. Children, widows, mothers—youth crossed out of faces by lines of suffering and life's penalties. Tragedy and sadness, and always it is in the faces of the women that the suffering is more plainly written. The men suffer in body—the women in soul.

The men look resigned. Their spirit is gone. What is it that happens behind these grey walls that kills so completely?

The devotion of the prisoners is almost childish in its eagerness as they sit with their children, talking with their wives, here and there a lover with his sweetheart—all of them have written a compelling story in the book of life. But love is in this room, love unashamed. Why are sinners always loved? Why do sinners make such wonderful lovers? Perhaps it is compensation, as they call it. Love is paged by every eye here.

Children are playing around the floor. Their laughter is like a benediction. This is another improvement, this room. There are no longer bars to separate loved ones. Human nature improves, but the tragedy remains just as dramatic.

The cells where they sleep are old-fashioned, built by a monster or a maniac. No architect could do such a thing for human beings. They are built of hate, ignorance, and stupidity. I understand they are building a new prison, more sane, with far more understanding of human needs. Until then these poor wretches must endure these awful cells. I'd go mad there.

I notice quite a bit of freedom. A number of prisoners are strolling around the grounds while others are at work. The honour system is a great thing, gives a man a chance to hold self-respect.

They have heard that I am coming, and most of them seem to know me. I am embarrassed. What can I say? How can I approach them? I wave my hand merely. "Hello, folks!"

I decide to discard conversation. Be myself. Be comic. Cut up. I twist my cane and juggle my hat. I kick up my leg in back. I am on comic ground. That's the thing.

No sentiment, no slopping over, no morals—they are fed up with that. What is there in common between us? Our viewpoints are entirely different. They're in—I'm out.

They show me a cup presented by Sir Thomas Lipton, inscribed, "We have all made mistakes."

"How do we know but what some of you haven't?" I ask, humorously. It makes a hit. They want me to talk.

"Brother criminals and fellow sinners: Christ said, 'Let him who is without sin cast the first stone.' I cannot cast the stone, though I have compromised and thrown many a pie. But I cannot cast the first stone." Some got it. Others never will.

We must be sensible. I am not a hero worshipper of criminals and bad men. Society must be protected. We are greater in number than the criminals and have the upper hand. We must keep it; but we can at least treat them intelligently, for, after all, crime is the outcome of society.

The doctor tells me that but a few of them are criminals from heredity, that the majority had been forced into crime by circumstances or had committed it in passion. I notice a lot of evil-looking men, but also some splendid ones. I earnestly believe that society can protect itself intelligently, humanly. I would abolish prisons. Call them hospitals and treat the prisoners as patients.

It is a problem that I make no pretence of solving.

The death house. It is hideous. A plain, bare room, rather large and with a white door, not green, as I have been told. The chair—a plain wooden armchair and a single wire coming down over it. This is an instrument to snuff out life. It is too simple. It is not even dramatic. Just cold-blooded and matter of fact.

Some one is telling me how they watch the prisoner after he is strapped in the chair. Good God! How can they calmly plan with such exactness? And they have killed as many as seven in one day. I must get out.

Two men were walking up and down in a bare yard, one a short man with a pipe in his mouth, walking briskly, and at his side a warden. The keeper announces, shortly, "The next for the chair."

How awful! Looking straight in front of him and coming toward us, I saw his face. Tragic and appalling. I will see it for a long time.

We visit the industries. There is something ironical about their location with the mountains for a background, but the effect is good, they can get a sense of freedom. A good system here, with the wardens tolerant. They seem to understand. I whisper to one.

"Is Jim Larkin here?" He is in the boot department, and we go to see him for a moment. There is a rule against it, but on this occasion the rule is waived.

Larkin struts up. Large, about six feet two inches, a fine, strapping Irishman. Introduced, he talks timidly.

He can't stay, mustn't leave his work. Is happy. Only worried about his wife and children in Ireland. Anxious about them, otherwise fit.

There are four more years for him. He seems deserted even by his party, though there is an effort being made to have his sentence repealed. After all, he is no ordinary criminal. Just a political one.

He asks about my reception in England. "Glad to meet you, but I must get back."

Frank tells him he will help to get his release. He smiles, grips Frank's hand hard. "Thanks." Harris tells me he is a cultured man and a fine writer.

But the prison marked him. The buoyancy and spirit that must have gone with those Irish eyes are no more. Those same eyes are now wistful, where they once were gay. He hasn't been forgotten. Our visit has helped. There may be a bit of hope left to him.

We go to the solitary-confinement cell, where trouble makers are kept.

"This young man tried to escape, got out on the roof. We went after him," says the warden.

"Yes, it was quite a movie stunt," said the youngster. He is embarrassed. We try to relieve it.

"Whatever he's done, he's darn handsome," I tell the warden. It helps. "Better luck next time," I tell him. He laughs. "Thanks. Pleased to meet you, Charlie."

He is just nineteen, handsome and healthy. What a pity! The greatest tragedy of all. He is a forger, here with murderers.

We leave and I look back at the prison just once. Why are prisons and graveyards built in such beautiful places?

Next day everything is bustling, getting ready for the trip back to Los Angeles. I sneak out in the excitement and go to a matinée to see Marie Doro in "Lilies of the Field," and that night to "The Hero," a splendid play. A young actor, Robert Ames, I believe, gives the finest performance I have ever seen in America.

We are on the way. I am rushing back with the swiftness of the Twentieth Century Limited. There is a wire from my studio manager. "When will I be back for work?" I wire him that I am rushing and anxious to get there. There is a brief stop in Chicago and then we are on again.

And as the train rushes me back I am living again this vacation of mine. Its every moment now seems wonderful. The petty annoyances were but seasoning. I even begin to like reporters. They are regular fellows, intent on their job.

And going over it all, it has been so worth while and the job ahead of me looks worth while. If I can bring smiles to the tired eyes in Kennington and Whitechapel, if I have absorbed and understood the virtues and problems of those simpler people I have met, and if I have gathered the least bit of inspiration from those greater personages who were kind to me, then this has been a wonderful trip, and somehow I am eager to get back to work and begin paying for it.

I notice a newspaper headline as I write. It tells of the Conference for Disarmament. Is it prophetic? Does it mean that War will never stride through the world again? Is it a gleam of intelligence coming into the world?

We are arriving at Ogden, Utah, as I write. There is a telegram asking me to dine with Clare Sheridan on my arrival in Los Angeles. The prospect is most alluring. And that wire, with several others, convinces me that I am getting home.

I turn again to the newspaper. My holiday is over. I reflect on disarmament. I wonder what will be the answer? I hope and am inclined to believe that it will be for good. Was it Tennyson who wrote:

When shall all men's good

Be each man's rule, and universal peace

Shine like a shaft of light across the lane,

And like a layer of beams athwart the sea?

What a beautiful thought! Can those who go to Washington make it more than a thought?

The conductor is calling:

"Los Angeles."

"Bye."

End of the book.

www.ingramcontent.com/pod-product-compliance
Lightning Source LLC
Chambersburg PA
CBHW071354310526
45790CB00017B/388